T0247744

CAN
SCHOOLS
SAVE
DEMOCRACY?

CAN SCHOOLS SAVE DEMOCRACY?

Civic Education
and the Common Good

Michael J. Feuer

Johns Hopkins University Press

BALTIMORE

Johns Hopkins University Press
2715 North Charles Street
Baltimore, Maryland 21218
www.press.jhu.edu

Library of Congress Cataloging-in-Publication Data

Names: Feuer, Michael J., author.
Title: Can schools save democracy? : civic education and the common good /
    Michael J. Feuer.
Description: Baltimore : Johns Hopkins University Press, 2023. |
    Includes bibliographical references and index.
Identifiers: LCCN 2023003671 | ISBN 9781421447773 (hardcover) |
    ISBN 9781421447780 (ebook)
Subjects: LCSH: Civics—Study and teaching—United States. |
    Democracy and education—United States. | Common good.
Classification: LCC LC1091 .F48 2023 | DDC 370.11/5—dc23/
    eng/20230224
LC record available at https://lccn.loc.gov/2023003671

A catalog record for this book is available from the British Library.

*Special discounts are available for bulk purchases of this book. For more information,
please contact Special Sales at specialsales@jh.edu.*

To Regine, Sarah, Jonathan, Emily, Kima,
and Hugo

And to good people everywhere
who stand for democracy and the common good

We have always known that heedless self-interest was bad morals, we now know that it is bad economics.

—Franklin D. Roosevelt

At war
Or at peace,
More people die
Of unenlightened self-interest
Than of any other disease

—Octavia Butler

CONTENTS

★ ★ ★

INTRODUCTION
EDUCATION AND DEMOCRACY

A RIDDLE FROM JEWISH FOLKLORE asks about the difference between optimists and pessimists. The mischievous answer is that pessimists have more data. I was reminded of this wry bit of wisdom while thinking of different takes on the condition of community life, civic responsibility, and prospects for democracy in America and elsewhere. On the gloomy side, for example, we have Robert Putnam, a distinguished political scientist who gained academic and popular acclaim with his book *Bowling Alone*, a data-enriched expansion of the argument he had published earlier in the *Journal of Democracy*. For Putnam, who would later be elected to the National Academy of Sciences and who relied in part on reputable data sources such as the General Social Survey, "something has happened in America in the last two or three decades to diminish civic engagement and social connectedness." His compelling image to make the case, people bowling solo instead of how they used to, in leagues, has become iconic for our fragmented and isolated times.[1]

Twenty-plus years later, as we confront daily reminders of a fierce tribalism that gnaws at sane democratic governance, Putnam seems prescient. Indeed, the notion of commitment to a democratic vision of the common good seemed quaint to many of us, if not absurd, as we watched congressional hearings with lurid reports and video images of the January 6 attack on the Capitol, as anti-maskers protested the alleged tyranny of government mandates, as right-leaning politicians fastened themselves to an "election-denial" fantasy, and as eminent scientists were mocked for their advice on how to curb infectious diseases of various strains.

Many authors and commentators have joined Putnam's league. *New York Times* columnist Michelle Goldberg noted that "there have been so many books about Trump and the fallout from Trumpism that the Pulitzer Prize–winning Washington Post book critic, Carlos Lozada, has written a book about all the Trump books. 'More political books have sold across all formats during this presidential term than at any point in NPD BookScan history,' said a recent report from the leading data company for U.S. book sales." Essays by Barton Gelman and George Packer in the *Atlantic* amplified the anxiety, and at the start of 2022 three new books warned of the imminent collapse of the America so many of us thought we knew (or at least wanted to believe in), all warning of impending civil war.[2]

The dire prognostications may seem exaggerated, but their ring has validity as three trends have converged. First, for decades Americans have been urged to believe that "civil service" is, at best, an oxymoron. The clever rhetoric of "government as the problem, not the solution," made famous by President Ronald Reagan in the early 1980s—an avowed conservative whose views today would place him closer to the political center—fueled decades of demagoguery in and out of the halls of Congress, fomented incivility in discourse, and rendered little service.

More recently, though, mainline pro-market philosophy that espoused limited government and the virtues of individual choice—which had legitimate theoretical grounding going back to the writings of Edmund Burke, Friedrich Hayek, Milton Friedman, and others—has been hijacked by a new breed of hardliners whose views are decidedly friendlier to the strong arm of state authority. The sustained assault on principled conservatism upended a legitimate and classically liberal distrust for government and propelled, albeit selectively, new attacks on personal freedoms that had been codified in decades of federal law and higher-court rulings. Efforts to minimize the role of government in curbing climate change, for example, may be seen as another instance of the more traditional "government off our backs" strain in American political and economic culture. But challenging the validity of elections, mistreating immigrants and migrants, overturning the fifty-year federal protection of women's reproductive rights, and banning books from classrooms and libraries are symptoms of an autocratic streak that leaves at least some conservative politicians (and everyone to their left) more than anxious.

The third strand in this knot of anti-democracy is a strident and abusive rhetoric that pollutes what was once a

noble airspace of political discourse and leaves even the most
dedicated partisans aghast. In a transformation that some analysts trace to Congressman Newt Gingrich and his acolytes
in the 1990s, bolstered by the Tea Party of the early 2000s
and inflamed by irresponsible and uncurated media outlets,
opponents are now labeled as *enemies*, and what was once healthy
democratic disagreement has turned into a blood sport,
metaphorically and physically.[3]

Universality is a weak form of therapy, but it is worth noting that we are not alone. The Social Science Research
Council published a set of articles about the global malaise,
and a European think tank wrote that the United States is
one of several countries to have experienced "backsliding,"
defined as "the sustained and deliberate process of subver-
sion of basic democratic tenets by political actors and governments." Anne Applebaum's analysis of what she calls "the lure
of authoritarianism" focuses on trends in Europe, especially
Hungary, Poland, and the United Kingdom. Efforts by Israel's
far-right coalition, elected in late 2022, to overhaul laws governing relations between the executive and judicial branches
and enact other extremist policies, led to the most difficult constitutional crisis in the country's seventy-five-year history. Examples of literature on the fragility of democracy include
essays in prominent scientific journals as well as in books by
distinguished historians and other academic researchers.[4]

And yet, all that data-informed pessimism notwithstanding, I see evidence of a resurgent, resilient, and, dare
I say, resplendent streak in the American ethos. I admit to
some confirmation bias here, to an impulsive embrace of
counterfactuals that tell a story of communal caring, per-

sonal sacrifice, and the durability of our democratic fabric. As an avid fan of the NBC *Nightly News*, I am buoyed by Lester Holt's standard signoff: "Take care of yourselves—and each other." Who isn't moved by the footage of apartment dwellers in Manhattan coming out of their pandemic prisons onto fire escapes to serenade ambulances taking victims of COVID-19 to overcrowded emergency rooms? Or the scenes of Vietnamese survivors of 1975 helping victims of the traumatic migration from Afghanistan in 2021 settle in the United States? In the wake of the murder of George Floyd and other victims of racial violence, public protest was the largest, most diverse, and most sustained in American history: Doesn't that suggest something even vaguely promising about our collective pursuit of justice and our appreciation for the role of civil protest in our ever-evolving democratic experiment? (Looking again to outside the United States, scenes of mass demonstrations by Israelis protesting their government's threats to undo the stunning success of the Zionist project provide another "light unto nations" struggling against the temptations of autocracy.)

That so much of the scary news in the United States is reported in our still-free press and that so many organizations have arisen against the would-be autocrats gives me hope. As the Brookings Institution analyst Elaine Kamarck observed, "Never before have we had a president who schemed to overturn legitimate election results, who attacked the press and the civil servants who worked for him, who admired dictators, who blatantly profited from his public office and who repeatedly lied to the public for his own selfish purposes . . . [and yet] . . . *the guardrails of democracy held. The institutions designed to check autocracy are intact*" (italics added). In a *Washington Post* column aptly titled "In the Capitol Nightmare, Democracy Prevailed," E. J. Dionne opined that "in the first week of January 2021, Trumpism, a movement that sought to undermine our democracy, was defeated, discredited and permanently shamed." The political scientist William Galston noted: "Not only did our institutions hold, but the most determined effort by a president to overturn the people's verdict in American history really didn't get anywhere. . . . It's not that it fell short. It didn't get anywhere." Reading these and other commentaries, I joined my brothers and sisters of all faiths in sighing to myself, *inshallah* (Arabic for "if God wills").[5]

From my vantage point as dean of an education school of roughly 1,400 students and 150 faculty and staff, in a university smacked by the pandemic with the worst financial and organizational crisis in its two-hundred-year history, I have data—not as quantitatively robust as those in the General Social Survey but revealing nonetheless—of community cohesion and a ferocious determination to "keep the wheels on the bus." The transition to remote instruction may not have been seamless, but student, faculty, and staff responses to surveys confirm personal fortitude along with an abiding concern for others' well-being. In the elementary and secondary school world, pupils, with their teachers, parents, and administrators, worked together—*together*, albeit virtually and certainly not without conflict—and made the best of an obviously dreadful situation. That "Zoom" made it into the *Oxford English Dictionary* "words of the year" is a sign of widespread determination to maintain social contact, sustain at least some semblance of normalcy and productivity, and enable people to keep and nurture relationships with others. As I suggested in various talks during the awful days of 2020, the "three Rs" of American schooling went from reading, 'riting, and 'rithmetic to resilience, recovery, and reform. We kept safe physical distance but enjoyed our emotional closeness; we breathed alone but, in a way, bowled together.*

This may sound like my optometrist gave me rose-tinted lenses, and surely it will surprise (and annoy) the pessimists, but perhaps less so some of our most eloquent chroniclers of American life. Writing in the *Atlantic*, for example, Nicholas Lemann, not known for shyness in reporting unpleasant realities, offered a different take from the world of sport, noting that the number of kids in youth soccer—which thrives on parental and community engagement—doubled between 1985 and 1996 (the year Putnam's first article appeared). Lemann aptly titled his critique "Kicking in Groups," to suggest that maybe more bowlers were playing alone but other athletes (and their families) still apparently believe in teamwork. For a more thorough and sustained vision, I am grateful to journalists James Fallows and Deborah Fallows for their book *Our Towns*, published in 2018. This narrated visit across America conjures a mosaic of cultural and political diversity, people and places coming to terms with local realities in their own ways but sharing a familiarly common recipe of engagement and generosity. *Our Towns* has since become the base for a network of initiatives about social capital, communal commitment, and the civic good—now more relevant

---

* I am grateful to my colleague Lionel Howard for suggesting an even better third R, *reimagination*.

than ever thanks to COVID-19, the convergent pandemic of racial violence, the trauma of global climate change, and the upheavals of economic disruption.[6]

So, back to the riddle: who has the data right? Researchers will continue the debate, which is fine because we need rigorous inquiry to substantiate (or dispel) impressions from selected stories. Bowling vs. soccer won't cut it when it comes to useful policy analysis. Meanwhile, though, other issues warrant attention as we continue to make sense of the numbers. One question is about the *effects* of social capital, defined by Putnam as "features of social organization such as networks, norms, and social trust that facilitate coordination and cooperation for mutual benefit." Does it advance us toward valued outcomes such as expansion of educational opportunity, improvement of health care, increased longevity, reduced economic inequality, and progress toward racial justice? That question has long been of interest to social scientists and, at least since the pioneering work of James Coleman in the 1960s, in education especially. The sociologist Adam Gamoran and colleagues, for example, found limited and mixed effects of social capital on student outcomes: in a random-assignment study of schools with high proportions of low-income, Latinx children, they found positive effects of social capital on children's behavioral outcomes in first grade and no effects on academic achievement in third grade. (Hint: resources for schools, preparation and employment of high-quality teachers, parental educational attainment, and advanced instructional methods really do matter.)[7]

Let me go a step further. Communities in the United States that allowed redlining and where screaming hordes blocked school integration were full of social capital. So were country clubs that barred entry for Blacks, Jews, and women; areas where commercial interests caused (and continue to cause) environmental degradation; and neighborhoods where resistance to vaccines and masks increased the spread of the pandemic. The Proud Boys, one of the more despicable fringe groups of the extreme right that became famous for antisemitic and racist "you will not replace us" ravings, thrive on close bonds against perceived common enemies. Indeed, social capital seems to be distributed bimodally. It is evident in places where the rich restrict entry to their gated neighborhoods, pay for their children to attend expensive schools, and otherwise enjoy being in the "top 1 percent." It is evident also in communities of the most severely disenfranchised and dislocated who are vulnerable to demagogues claiming to represent their interests in a "populist" agenda.

My point here is certainly not that strengthening of social capital would be a bad thing. But it's not enough to have bonds *within* groups that do not automatically translate to meaningful bonds *across* groups. Nor is social capital synonymous with moral rectitude: let's not forget the ugly truth about collective collaboration and the spontaneous silence of socially connected neighbors and bystanders who enabled and fueled Nazi brutality. As documented in a brilliant podcast produced in late 2021 by *Tablet* magazine and hosted by journalist Andrew Lapin, Father Charles Coughlin—a Detroit-based former Canadian, a rabid antisemite and fan of Hitler, Goebbels, and Mussolini—became known as the "radio priest" with his show that attracted 30 million weekly listeners in the 1930s; his rallies at Madison Square Garden played

to masses obviously comfortable in their camaraderie. (Coughlin's demise is a hopeful reminder that America's occasional
flirtations with fascism have not yet gotten past second base.
May our good-luck streak continue or, as my grandmother
might have said, "*Hallevai*" [from the original Aramaic via Yid-
dish and Hebrew for "May it only be so."])[8]

Efforts to rebuild or reinforce social networks and political
participation—a hopeful antidote to the harms caused by
greedy self-interest and its extensions to tribal extremism—
will not be adequate to preserve traditions of democracy or
advance us toward egalitarian aspirations. What's often missing in the discussion about community cohesion is rules—an
agreed-upon set of political, legal, moral, and economic
principles and values that govern and delimit human behavior. Without greater appreciation for the origins and meanings of agreed-upon constraints needed to make social life
possible, and acceptance of the need to enforce them, pursuit of individual or community preferences risks becoming
the fuel that pollutes the public good. Put differently, unregulated accumulation of capital, whether financial or social,
may benefit some lucky citizens but often imposes painful and
unacceptable costs on the rest of us. In the pages that follow,
my discussion of social self-control and the acceptance of
carefully circumscribed limits on individualism (and what
might be called "small-group-ism"), especially in a society that
has long privileged personal freedom over group preferences,
branches off from traditional legal reasoning and is rooted in
theories of collective action and public economics.

WHAT IS CIVICS?

Which brings me to the central questions that motivate this book:

1. What types of collective rules and norms of mutual self-regulation are most salient to the healthy functioning of democracy in pluralist societies?
2. How can a greater number of people learn about those rules and become prepared to apply them in their personal life, work, and communities?

I approach these questions, which are familiar to students of history, law, economics, sociology, psychology, public policy, moral philosophy, and politics, with three perhaps naïve assumptions. First, thinking again about optimism and pessimism, I believe there is a safe middle ground, a platform upon which we might neither scoff at the bad news nor skid into utter despair, and from which we might begin to organize knowledge and action to rebuild traditions of civic responsibility. In other words, rather than wait for proof about exactly how bad things are and postpone action until we have "clinched" that debate once and for all, can we agree there is room for improvement and try to make things at least marginally better in our lifetimes?[9]

My second assumption, or caveat, is that finding the middle ground and agreeing on a set of principles and their application requires respectful argument and willingness to compromise. It is already clear that renewed public and professional advocacy for civics, like so much else in American political life, vocalizes divergent assumptions and aspirations. It is less clear how to tune that cacophony into something more harmonious, and whether we can realistically aim for agreement on at least a baseline set of principles. As a first approximation to answering the question "What is civics, anyway?" the summary of a recent conference cosponsored by ETS and Educating for American Democracy is on point: see box 1 for a definition that appeals to me because it includes— and blends—knowledge, skills, dispositions, and engagement.

 BOX 1. CIVIC COMPETENCIES

- *Knowledge*: understanding of governments in the United States and in other nations, along with understanding of related social studies concepts, including the effects of history on current governments and societies
- *Skills*: ability to engage actively and effectively in democratic processes by applying skills such as critical thinking, teamwork, written and oral communication, and information literacy
- *Dispositions*: attitudes that support democratic participation, including an appreciation of the responsibilities of citizenship, interest in the welfare of others, a sense of personal and collective agency, and capacity to engage in civil disagreement while maintaining civic friendship
- *Engagement*: integration of knowledge, skills, and dispositions to solve public problems, improve communities and societies, and navigate formal and informal political systems and processes; can occur individually or collectively and encompasses civic actions and civic participation.

★ *Source*: Abridged from Hamilton and Parsi 2022.

Now, it might be argued that if we already had what it takes to pursue (and reach) a consensus over such a definition, and more specifically over a set of mutually acceptable constraints on social and economic interactions, and if we were willing to relax our ideological certainties for the sake of civil discourse and the common good, that might mean we don't need to worry about all this in the first place. I'd love to be shown that everything is fine, thank you, and that the push for revived civic education is a waste of time. Alas, current events nudge me back into the more pessimistic corner.

My third assumption, more a hope, really, is that I'm not too late, that by the time this book is published we will still have a functioning "moral democracy"—a working system of representative government that advances us toward the vision enshrined in our founding documents—and that we are ready to experiment with ideas for making it even more moral and even more functional. A bit of prayer at this point couldn't hurt.[10]

WHAT'S INSIDE

The argument in this book builds on two connected pillars. First, I join with other proponents of civic education as a necessary, albeit insufficient, strategy for a course correction needed to preserve democracy. I use the singular, *civic* education, to denote strategies for engaging the worlds of business, government, media, philanthropy, and the schools, in a set of principles or rules for healthy democracy. I use the plural, *civics* education, for the teaching and learning of those principles in formal classroom settings. Civic education needs to be "holistic," a core pursuit in all of education, in school and out, and the use of different tools and methods at different times to achieve various goals with diverse populations across all ages.

Civic education needs to be theoretical, didactic, and active. Increasingly widespread anxiety about the present danger is reflected in a burgeoning scholarly and popular literature that either laments real threats, with frightening historical evidence, but is mostly light on what to do about it, or pleads for on-the-ground action, typically to advance specific political agendas and visions of social cohesion with little conceptual grounding to guide teaching and public understanding. As is often the case, many advocates favor consensus as long their specific viewpoints are well represented. My goal here is to go from describing scary trends to outlining a program, anchored in a revived curriculum to be implemented at the high school level, which will slow, if not arrest, the erosion of civility and the demise of democracy. As I hope to show, reenergizing the high school curriculum will be a catalyst for developing new approaches for reaching a general public, a topic which I address mainly in chapter 4.

I noted earlier that there are three converging threats to democracy: overzealous faith in free choice and markets and disdain for government-sponsored collective action, the concentration of government power in the hands of would-be autocrats, and the erosion of civil discourse between political partisans. Most of my argument in this book centers on the first of those hazards, though I believe that real progress requires attention to their combined toxicity. Fortunately (or not), problems of authoritarianism and the demise of respectful argumentation are topics covered more fully in a growing scholarly and journalistic literature.

As hinted by the book's subtitle, then, my focus is on the "common good," a concept that involves understanding the tensions between personal rights and social wrongs and defining the criteria by which to evaluate the acceptability of economic and social arrangements that are ineluctably imperfect. The proposed road map for curriculum reform is anchored in theories of political economy, public goods, and collective action. A central idea in this discussion is the specter of undesirable outcomes—"tragedies of the commons"—which necessitates consideration of how democracies design, manage, and enforce economic, legal, and political arrangements. Though intuitively obvious even to readers without formal training in philosophy, law, or political economy, appreciation for the role of democratically elected government in protecting society from even the most well-intentioned actions of its members sadly has become inaudible in public discourse, muffled by the drone of rhetoric that exalts the rationality of free choice and spreads panic about government overreach. (These concepts are also not a salient feature of most social studies and civics education, as I document later.)[11]

I concentrate on this slice of the bigger civic education pie in response to disturbing trends in the United States (with parallels elsewhere), chief among them a palpable disdain for government, even among those serving in high elected and appointed positions; erosion of trust in science and objective inquiry; resurgence of racism, antisemitism, misogyny, nativism, and other forms of bigotry; and the gleeful willingness of certain politicians to succumb to temptations of totalitarianism. Those fault lines have always existed in our social geology, but they have become painfully more apparent during and after the concurrent pandemics of COVID-19, racial violence, climate change, and economic disruption. Let me elaborate: much of my reasoning about individual rights and social outcomes derives from a critique of anti-governmentalism (to coin a phrase). It is clear, though, that current threats to democracy are fueled also by people with autocratic and narcissistic impulses—that is, by people with a talent for aggrandizement of, rather than limitation of, government power over the lives of individuals. Traditional "conservativism," which, even in its less libertarian extremist versions, cautioned against bureaucratic overreach, has been at least somewhat overtaken by politicians determined to interfere with individual rights for the sake of ideological and religious dogma. Still, in this complex environment of political and cultural turbulence, I am arguing for a focus on public goods and the fragility of markets, which, hopefully will have long-term value assuming the "lure of authoritarianism" continues to be resisted.

Amid turbulence over the meanings and methods of democracy, public anxiety grows about the quality of education. Indeed, it is not uncommon to hear people blame schools and colleges—where many of the perpetrators spent much of their youth—for the January 6 assault on the Capitol, the resurgence of racist and antisemitic hate crimes, and the spread of wild conspiracy theories about everything from voter fraud to computer chips in vaccines to the "hoax" of climate change. This is not a new phenomenon. In the United States and elsewhere, the condition of schooling looms large during periods of economic strain and social unrest.

Whether and how much the formal education sector is responsible for the current crisis, and how reforms in curriculum and school governance might arrest or reverse forces that gnaw at the fabric of democracy, are complicated questions. It is customary to blame the K–12 system for a host of problems: perceived threats to economic competitiveness and national security, rising crime and urban violence, stagnant wage growth, declining social mobility, and disappearance of the middle class. And when partisan politics reaches seemingly boundless ferocity, colleges and universities come in for an especially rough drubbing, with partisans of both left and right eager to prove that their perspectives are awash in storms of political correctness. Although much of the scapegoating rests on shaky empirical foundations, it would be equally wrong to exempt the education establishment from any responsibility in equipping future leaders with knowledge and skills relevant to the preservation of democratic ideals.[12]

Schools need to be a part of the action, *but not the only part*. Given the level of interest in the condition of education post-COVID-19, anticipated teacher shortages, and heated arguments about curriculum, we are at a rare moment of interest in the possibility of national and international cooperation on civic-oriented education reform. How can we engage high schools and colleges, simultaneously and sequentially, in revising and reenergizing civic learning focused on individual choice and social values and connecting the education sector to leaders and influencers in business, government, media, and philanthropy? As I suggest later, our capacity for reinforcing those connections is limited by the tensions that make them ever more important. The forces tugging at the fabric of democracy, which give rise to calls for improved education, are the same ones that prevent rational discourse and the acceptance of consensus on what should be taught to whom and in what settings. (If you're not sure what I mean, go to a meeting of your local school board and listen in on the debate over whether and how to integrate the history of slavery in high school social studies.)

My proposed model builds on links between the K–12 and postsecondary sectors: how colleges and universities articulate expectations for student qualifications and predictions of their success affects the quality and content of teaching and learning precollege; and vice versa, what is taught in high school sets the stage for college and graduate school instruction. If organizationally it makes sense to compartmentalize education into K–12 and postsecondary, such efficiency blurs appreciation for their inherent connections. I will argue that *teacher education* can connect activities aimed at bolstering civic knowledge and skills, for four reasons (figure 1). First, preparation of future educators has direct effects, albeit delayed, on how high school civics is taught. Giving prospective teachers an enriched program of study that includes core principles of democratic governance—especially those related to collective action and public goods—should become the basis for improved instruction when they begin (or continue) their classroom experiences.*

---

* I am grateful to Mike Usdan for suggesting I expand the model to include the earlier grades, based on the astute observation that high school may be too late. But I'm afraid I'll just have to leave that to the sequel, whether written by me or others. On the other hand, Mike's endorsement of my effort here to connect the K–12 and postsecondary sectors is much appreciated. See, e.g., Kirst et al. (2011).

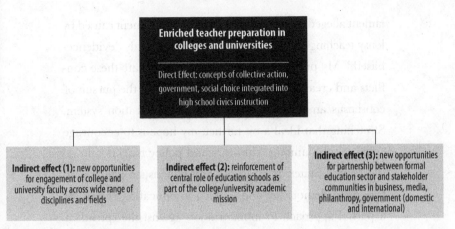

FIGURE 1. Logic model for new civic education program

Second, how future educators are prepared—especially in institutions of higher education, where most teachers and school leaders learn their craft and gain certification—can have indirect effects, by stimulating interactions among students majoring in education and their peers preparing for careers in science, business, government, and the arts. An enriched program would therefore involve scholars from a wide range of fields and disciplines not typically part of the teacher preparation enterprise. This would be revolutionary in many research-intensive universities, where opportunities for cross-disciplinary collaboration connected to teacher professional development are rare.

Third, possibilities for catalytic effects of teacher preparation on campus extend to improved ties outside the ivory tower. Much of the discourse on the role of education in economy and society bubbles with hostile rhetoric in both directions: educators feel threatened by the intrusion of "outsiders" in their pedagogy, and leaders in business and science lament alleged stagnation in academic achievement caused by lousy teaching cluttered with methods not exactly "evidence-based." My proposed strategy aims to attenuate these conflicts and create an atmosphere conducive to the pursuit of consensus among "stakeholders" in the education system. Stretching that ideal a bit further, my hope is to encourage collaboration among educators and policy makers outside the United States, in countries and regions struggling with threats to democracy and looking to education reform as a partial approach to immunization against the spread of authoritarianism.

Finally, although most teacher professional development takes place in colleges and universities, it is increasingly challenged by alternative pathways to licensure that are touted as more efficient, less mired in outdated academic norms, and more interesting intellectually. Without attempting to adjudicate such claims, which are fraught with partisan fever and mostly unburdened by hard evidence, the program outlined here should be relevant across the complex ecology of educator professional development. Again, I stop short of prescribing specific pedagogies, but offer ideas for consideration by experienced teachers and curriculum designers.

The book is organized as follows. In chapter 1, I review highlights of a long (ageless?) discussion of theories of individual rights, collective action, and social outcomes. The chapter is a kind of primer on contributions of economic theory that builds on a basic assumption: regulated *democratic* capitalism has brought more benefits to more of humanity than any other system, but adherence to orthodoxy about "rational self-interest" and distrust of government increases the magnitude and spread of harmful social outcomes. Against the backdrop of growing autocratic tendencies—centralization of power and denial of basic individual and human rights—my logic is fundamentally more optimistic in its underlying expectation and hope that principles of freedom will somehow prevail. Hence, I focus on a "commons" logic that hinges on concepts of individual choice and that can enrich public understanding of familiar dilemmas—resistance to vaccination against various infectious diseases, tensions between religious freedom and public health, climate change, public funding of scientific research, hazards of uncurated social media, and the role of private philanthropy in advancing the public interest. A key part of my argument is that the "tragedy of the commons" is *not* our inevitable destiny, but rather that it can open our minds (and hearts) to the development of policies to prevent the most dismal outcomes.[13]

To what extent does contemporary civics instruction in American schools, and perhaps elsewhere, already address that cluster of problems? As I suggest in chapter 2, the short answer is "not enough." Based on an abridged review of the history of civics and "citizenship" as core elements of public schooling, I argue that as important as those ideas were to the shaping of American education, they were almost always treated as byproducts of courses in government, history, and the social studies; in the lingo of education, the concepts were rarely "curricularized," but understood as valued outcomes of other more traditional subjects.

In addition, I argue that regardless of whether and where civics may have had its niche in the crowded school curriculum, it has suffered a downgrading largely to make room for more intensive focus on science and mathematics instruction. This pattern reflects a pendulum swing in American education philosophy, from what the historian Carl Kaestle referred to as the "political functions of schools," dominant in eighteenth- and nineteenth-century thinking, to a post–World War II emphasis on the "economic functions of schools." I look at selected contemporary syllabi used in university-based teacher education to show where there is room for inclusion of principles of political economy—not only in the social studies, history, and the humanities, but also in STEM subjects (science, technology, engineering, and mathematics). For the latter, I am especially interested in possibilities for integration that do not inflame tensions between advocates for more teaching of science and mathematics and advocates for more teaching of the humanities.[14]

Chapter 3 then attempts a more concrete road map for curriculum reform, with examples that bring to life the subtleties of public goods and collective action theory, some of which were hinted at in the preceding chapter. The goal in chapter 3 is not to design a curriculum—well beyond my expertise—but rather to offer themes that teachers and administrators might translate into syllabi and instructional modules; to make the case that those themes are worthy of inclusion in the preparation of future teachers in schools of education; and to suggest that to do that well, college-based educator preparation programs should invite new collaborations with colleagues in the physical, behavioral, and social sciences. Good educator preparation requires a blend of pedagogical knowledge (the wheelhouse of teacher educators) and content knowledge (drawing from economics, political theory, sociology, psychology, law, and the other relevant disciplines).[15]

In chapter 4, I return to the argument that although schools must be part of the action to save democracy, they can't go it alone: public education means not just what takes place in school but as importantly how the general public is educated, in this case about democracy and its frailties. Readers of John Dewey will recognize the idea that the bridge connecting schools and their surroundings carries two-way traffic. Preparing adults for productive participation in complex pluralist systems hinges on active engagement and support of political, business, media, and philanthropic stakeholders. Links between schools and the "outside world" have been essential to emerging concepts of "accountability," and require negotiated terms of endearment between educators and the general public.

Designing viable partnerships between schools and their external communities, therefore, will model the healthy pluralism to which we aspire. In a word, preaching (and teaching) civics is insufficient if we don't practice it. To advance these arguments I reference successful examples such as the advent of "research-practice partnerships" that connect school districts to university-based expertise; university-industry "roundtables" that reinforce ties between laboratory research and technology development/diffusion; increasing reliance on private philanthropy to support basic and applied research; and connections between university-based scholars and think tanks that work with mainstream media and community-based advocates to promote evidence-informed policy deliberations. I then extend the logic to cross-national collaborations, with an eye toward supplanting counterproductive competition (e.g., the race for higher PISA rankings) with a collective spirit energized by mutual trust.

The final chapter is a short summary and postscript. I restate the central arguments and offer a final word of optimistic caution: the gears of democracy and education continue to grind, as they must, and our challenge is and will continue to be to find enough hope to sustain resilience and pursue progress.

FREE TO BRUISE

POLITICAL ECONOMY
AND THE LIMITS OF LIBERTY

Freedom for the wolves has often meant
death for the sheep.

ISAIAH BERLIN

There is no example on record of someone
voluntarily washing a rented car.

ANONYMOUS

AMERICANS ARE A RELIGIOUS PEOPLE, in the sense of formal
affiliation as well as personal connectedness to God, which
often surprises visitors from abroad where separation of
church and state is defined and enforced differently. In western Europe, government sponsorship of religion seems to have
had little effect on personal faith and engagement: most people
identify as Christian, but few (about 20 percent) regularly go

to church. In the United States, where the Constitution prohibits state "establishment," the attendance rate is almost double. Also somewhat surprising is that religious affiliation is not a strong predictor of political preferences: almost 40 percent of evangelical Protestants and 70 percent of Catholics in the United States say that homosexuality should be accepted, and 30 and 60 percent, respectively, accept same-sex marriage. Complexities of religion in the public sphere are beyond the scope of this book. But one thing is clear: religious fanaticism is not how most Americans define their creed or approach the ballot box (at least not yet).[1]

In economics and social policy, though, an orthodox streak runs deep. Adherence to theories of free markets, based more on faith than data and more pervasive among ideologues with traditionally conservative philosophies than the masses, has been a bulwark against government's role in activities that other nations assume are the province of the state. Passage of landmark advances such as Social Security, Medicare, environmental protection, occupational safety, federal funding of basic science, student loans, and the Affordable Care Act were outliers, heralded for their defiance of demagogues fanning the flames about socialism and social engineering. How many presidential election campaigns have been dominated by arguments for lowering taxes to leave money in the hands of working families to manage their own choices? How many votes do candidates lose for suggesting we mimic the protective social safety nets of Scandinavia or France? Throughout much of the twentieth century, and with added fervency in the last fifty years, the drone of pro-market zealots has stifled awareness of the concept of "public goods" and distracted civic-minded Americans from appreciating that reliance on the miracle of markets may not always serve their best interests.[2]

But nothing in the American system is without anomalies. Although the argument for a strong government role in providing or at least regulating certain economic activities is always heated, and the "dance of legislation" is often unbearably slow, majorities of the population often support the result. When enlightened leaders convey the rationale and advantages of government involvement in selected activities, most Americans usually get the point and become resolute in not turning back the clock. Indeed, a good way to *lose* votes in national elections is to threaten privatization of cherished government programs. A public opinion poll in 2019 showed that 70 percent of respondents regard Social Security favorably and 33 percent very favorably, with only 6 percent viewing it very unfavorably. Democrats usually tilt toward policy that acknowledges and honors the role of government, Republicans toward solutions that rely on the private sector; but when we had a sane moderate center, partisans on both sides of the proverbial aisle were willing to meet midway in pursuit of balanced and pragmatic problem-solving. (Granted, even our "sane moderate center" was not immune from the scourge of racist, sexist, homophobic, antisemitic, and xenophobic extremism.)[3]

In a way, then, the politics of federal intervention inverts the logic of religious establishment. Just as belief in God seems to be inversely correlated with government involvement, and efforts to relax antiestablishment rules meet strong opposition, Americans' reliance on public policy is firm—albeit selectively—in the face of persistent and nagging rhetoric by government officials touting the need to shrink the size of the public sector. Still, the burden of proof more typically falls on advocates for the federal role. We saw this phenomenon again in early 2022 during the debate over voting rights legislation and the filibuster. A distinguished Republican senator opined that "the federal government must [not] urgently displace centuries of constitutional practice that gives states primary control over elections." To which a leading civil rights activist argued that "when it comes to constitutional rights such as voting, the federal role needs to be unequivocal." That seemingly perpetual argument reflects a strand of American "exceptionalism" etched in the philosophical pillars of the new republic: the revolutionary idea that government exists to serve the people and not the other way around, a chronic allergy to centralized authority, and our codified (if still unfulfilled) guarantee of individual rights. Our romantic fascination with entrepreneurship distinguishes us from countries where proposals to privatize prisons, air traffic control, or education would be viewed with a mix of wonder and horror. (P.S.: The voting rights bill failed.)[4]

Pragmatism reinforces the American cultural and ideological preference for privatization. Years ago, in reviewing a book that argued for "regulation everywhere," I quipped that the ordeal of buying a bottle of wine in a "state store" in Philadelphia, operating under the weight of the Pennsylvania Liquor Control Board and its Kafkaesque regulations, was enough to drive people to drink. Humor aside, I would venture that most Americans consider themselves lucky to live in a society that prides efficiency and innovation over gummy bureaucracy. They are on to something: quality of life improved steadily for most Americans through at least the first three-quarters of the twentieth century, at which point sharply rising income inequality began to reverse progress (here and around the industrialized world). Intergenerational social mobility slowed, but rumors of the death of the middle class and the end of the "American dream" are exaggerated. In 2018, only Luxembourg and Singapore, among ten rapidly developing countries, had higher gross domestic product per capita than the United States (figure 2).[5]

Other indicators echo the basic point: until recently, higher education enrollment and completion rates were higher in the

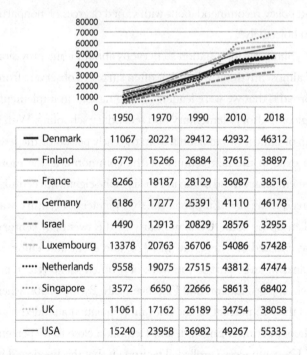

	1950	1970	1990	2010	2018
▬ Denmark	11067	20221	29412	42932	46312
▬ Finland	6779	15266	26884	37615	38897
▬ France	8266	18187	28129	36087	38516
▬▬▬ Germany	6186	17277	25391	41110	46178
▬ ▬ Israel	4490	12913	20829	28576	32955
▬ ▬ Luxembourg	13378	20763	36706	54086	57428
••••• Netherlands	9558	19075	27515	43812	47474
••••• Singapore	3572	6650	22666	58613	68402
••••• UK	11061	17162	26189	34754	38058
▬▬ USA	15240	23958	36982	49267	55335

FIGURE 2. GDP per capita, selected countries, 1950–2018, in 2011 US$
Source: Based on the author's computations of data from the Maddison Project Database 2020. The full database can be found at https://www.rug.nl/ggdc/historicaldevelopment/maddison/releases/maddison-project-database-2020.

United States than in much of the rest of the Western world, where attendance is "free" thanks to heavy state subsidies. It is not blind chauvinism to celebrate American colleges and universities as the envy of many nations in terms of student experience, research productivity, and contributions to the public welfare. The idea of academic independence from the federal government, in our complex ecology of public and private colleges and universities, is a hallmark of the American system. It is bolstered by a remarkable and growing "advice sector" with more than 2,000 think tanks and research organizations contributing empirical analysis, evaluation of public programs, and policy recommendations with varied degrees of nonpartisan objectivity.[6]

Similarly, for a nation so nervous about public provision of almost anything, a fact that often surprises observers from abroad is that we were leaders among nations in implementing compulsory elementary and secondary schooling. With a gap of almost two millennia from the early period of the Jewish exile in the first century of the common era, the more contemporary trend began in Prussia in the eighteenth century, spread to western Europe in the mid-nineteenth century, was taken up by some US states early in the twentieth century, was codified in federal law in 1920, and eventually enforced thanks in large part to the work of women social reformers such as Jane Addams and Florence Kelly. By the 1950s, when less than 15 percent of the relevant population attended high school in France, England, and Denmark, close to 80 percent of US youth were enrolled. The irony is that this happened in a place where, as a former president of Harvard once wrote, "We don't really have an education *system* but rather a *chaos*." It took 214 years to pass "national goals" for education—which to this day are viewed with suspicion and have had little influence on policy and practice. Its many imperfections notwithstanding, public education financed and governed primarily at the state and local levels—at present there are roughly 15,000 independent school districts operating under authority of 50-plus states—is still the modal choice for overwhelming majorities of Americans.[7]

Polling data provide familiar, if somewhat contradictory, findings: many Americans tend to like their neighborhood schools, but complain that the system needs repair and claim that in important ways public education is "off track." In any case, private independent and religious schools continue to serve fewer than 9 percent of the relevant age cohort; charter schools, partly freed from central bureaucracy, enroll roughly 5 percent. The key point is that "public" is a different and more accepted concept than "federal" in the American lexicon. Initiatives such as "the Common Core" for K–12 standards, although initiated at the state level with various professional societies, met resistance largely due to misinformation campaigns suggesting it was part of a federal takeover. We still privilege the *pluribus* even as we aspire to some kind of *unum*.[8]

Reticence to cede authority to the central government is reflected, too, in our exceptionalist philanthropic system. Instincts of individual generosity are bolstered by tax incentives that encourage families and foundations to invest in programs for the public good with limited accountability, and often in ways that contest the same government that authorizes the autonomy in the first place. Criticisms of our rules regarding charitable giving recur with almost cyclical regularity, and although they are often steeped in partisan ideology, the arguments warrant consideration. It is not obvious that opponents of private influence on school reform, such as provided by the Gates and other foundations, would be happy knowing that all school policies were to be the province of the Department of Education, especially in a right-leaning administration. In any case, my sense is that on balance more good than harm has come from a system that keeps some public money in private hands.[9]

And for a final example of why Americans are wary of so-called public options, here is one that may surprise readers: our peculiar system of health insurance—still organized (if that is the proper word for a system that appears hopelessly chaotic) through private enterprise more than government—is not the main cause of our low (and declining) life expectancy compared to countries with nationalized coverage. Our system is often blamed for the statistic that we spend more than other countries but enjoy less health, and there is some truth in that statement. But our grossly inefficient system, in which the transaction costs of figuring out what kind of insurance to buy or participate in, and negotiating ad nauseam with providers about anticipated reimbursements, is not largely responsible for our unhealthy health status. According to a 2001 report of the Institute of Medicine (now the National Academy of Medicine), "about 18,000 unnecessary deaths occur each year in the United States because of lack of health insurance." In contrast, though, the Centers for Disease Control and Prevention (CDC) reported that roughly 435,000 excess deaths occur each year *because of unhealthy behaviors.* This finding is echoed in more recent analyses, which show, for example, that smoking, alcohol consumption, drug abuse, unsafe sex, and poor exercise habits account for roughly 30 percent of measured health outcomes; another 40 percent is attributable to socioeconomic status and inequality; and 10 percent is caused by problems in the physical environment. Which leaves about 20 percent attributable to lack of access to good health care. One conclusion reached by social demographers studying these data is that "the health care system does not appear to be an important contributor to the low longevity ranking of the U.S." The real culprits, as suggested by the data summarized above, are massive inequality and an unconscionable child poverty level, thanks in large part to decades of market fundamentalism and concerted efforts to protect the uber-wealthy, and the persistent failure to discourage individual behaviors that are fundamentally hazardous. Expanding affordable access to high quality care is a legitimate policy goal, and fortunately the Affordable Care Act resulted in coverage for millions of previously uninsured Americans. That is a step to be applauded, even while acknowledging that fixing the insurance system alone will not have as much impact as investments in child care, education, workforce development, and programs to reduce substance abuse, obesity brought on by bad eating habits, smoking, violence, and other toxic behaviors. Meanwhile, to the extent that many Americans value the quality of medical care they get, it is understandable why efforts to dismantle the privately organized insurance system meet with skepticism if not resistance. (Note, though, that the tendency to engage in unhealthy behaviors may in fact be correlated with people's access to good quality care, which suggests that our insurance system may bear more responsibility for declining longevity than is apparent from the raw statistics.)[10]

My purpose here is not to settle the debate over free enterprise and its discontents or pinpoint where to set the dial on the scale of "rival views of market society." The complex American economic system gets mixed grades. As a first approximation, based on my reading of the data, *regulated* capitalism has brought more benefit to more people than any other system. *What worries me is what happens when people drop the qualifier adjective, when the fragile balance of individual rights and the public good is disrupted by extremists who perceive any collectively organized constraint on private behavior as a step on the road to tyranny.* The principles that need to be baked more thoroughly into syllabi of civics education and transmitted as widely as possible are (1) that seemingly rational self-interest seeking does not necessarily yield socially rational outcomes, and (2) that to protect capitalism and its followers from its own self-destruction, political intervention—a visible hand, sometimes coercive, sometimes as a more gentle "nudge" toward better outcomes—is required.[11]

The proper mix of public and private arrangements in democratic societies has been debated for centuries, not just by economists but also by political philosophers, psychologists, biologists, sociologists, and legal scholars. It is the essential topic of political economy, the study of how political and economic behavior, at the individual and macro levels, intersect and how to estimate the tradeoffs between individual and social benefits. If economics dominates many policy debates, it is in large part thanks to a robust analytical apparatus that enables empirical estimation of effects of alternative production and consumption systems. Undergirding the cathedral of so-called positive economics is a set of parsimonious assumptions leading to testable predictions which are applied widely even to issues that may not appear to be economic. For example, prohibiting smokers from lighting up in elevators, which infringes on the right of people to enjoy the benefits of tobacco, reflects a societal decision to protect innocent nonsmokers riding in the same car. That is first and foremost a health matter—data on secondhand smoke are now largely indisputable—but how to manage the risks is a legal, economic, and organizational question for which health professionals may not have the requisite set of skills and knowledge.

The smoking example is a classic case of *externalities*, defined as "spillover effects of decisions that fall on parties not otherwise involved in a market as a producer or a consumer of a good or service." The imagery is powerful because it generalizes to a larger class of situations that necessitate legal or other coercive arrangements that intrude on liberty; to borrow from Isaiah Berlin, freedom for smokers in elevators can bring death to the other passengers. Not surprisingly, some economists who have delved into these kinds of predicaments have offered a market-like solution: the possibility that people stuck in that elevator might negotiate a fair solution, either by smokers indemnifying nonsmokers or nonsmokers bribing smokers to hold off until they reach their floor, is addressed in the literature of the economics of property rights.[12]

GOING TO MARKET . . . AND BACK

It is not hard to draw a line connecting arguments for and against unregulated free enterprise, on the one hand, and arguments in favor of and opposed to collective action generally, on the other. Understanding the origins of these disputes is essential for civic-minded educators, in and out of the school system. Where to start? Among the most eloquent and evocative priests of capitalism in its purest form, Friedrich Hayek and Milton Friedman take top honors. They both won the Nobel Memorial Prize in Economic Sciences, Hayek in 1974 and Friedman in 1976, and along with colleagues in their respective institutions (notably the University of Chicago), their work erected a robust theoretical foundation for market solutions that found many eager believers. The title of this chapter plays on Friedman's famous (infamous?) manifesto *Free to Choose*, written with his spouse, Rose Friedman, which added a Nobelist's prestige to rhetoric that captivated a generation of free-marketeers and caused havoc in social and education policy in the United States, Chile, and elsewhere. Some commentators—including economists—have laid blame squarely on the supply side, blasting the "Chicago boys" who advocated for school vouchers and who egged on the banking sector in creating and then puncturing the mortgage bubble and causing global financial collapse. Although it is tempting to demonize suppliers of market dogma, it is important to remember the demand side: after all, the dismantling of public education in Chile could not have happened without substantial political "uptake." Conversely, it is worth noting, mercifully, that decades of hectoring by right-wing think tanks about the virtues of choice and competition have not yet been successful in destroying American public education.[13]

In any case, what is often missed in commentary about economists and the human condition is the profession's own preoccupation with the hazards of free enterprise. The best example is Adam Smith, the eighteenth-century genius (no, I'm not being sarcastic) whose insights about "the wealth of nations" were monumental. In his most-cited oeuvre (with that title) he made clear, to those who bothered to read the fine print, his views on the risks of private self-interest seeking and concentration of business power. In a less familiar but arguably more important book, aptly titled *The Theory of Moral Sentiments*, he underscored the need for *rules*. As noted on the website of the Adam Smith Institute, "We have a natural tendency to look after ourselves . . . [but we] have to work out how to live alongside others without doing them harm . . . we force [people] . . . to obey the *rules* of justice because society could not otherwise survive" (italics added). A cautious supporter of *laissez-faire*, Smith did not advocate, as many who like to cite him do, what might be called *laissez-aller* . . . as in letting competition and private business interests run amok.[14]

That tradition of caution about free enterprise remains strong; to the possible surprise of many popular critics, economics has produced a rigorous and voluminous literature on market *failure*. Granted, there is in much of that writing a subtle predisposition favoring (and viewing with awe) the magic of markets. But for every page of theory flaunting their virtues there are at least as many dense mathematical proofs of conditions under which markets are predicted to produce suboptimal social outcomes. In the classics of microeconomics, for example, chapters on the pure theory of consumption,

production, and equilibrium are followed by chapters covering imperfect competition, externalities, public goods, and the
aggregation of individual preferences into a conceptualiza-
tion of "social welfare." A staple of economic reasoning is
tradeoffs between efficiency and equity; self-interest and competition may yield positive benefits for some but need to be
weighed against the risks of rising inequality and the perpetuation of disadvantage for many. Another branch of research
emphasizes distortions when buyers and sellers have asym-
metric information, which has spawned a literature (and a
handful of Nobel prizes) applied to trade, labor relations, and
insurance systems. An eloquent, though sadly not as well-
known corpus of work by economist Albert Hirschman challenged much of the received gospel of economic theory, based
on the author's rare and sublime combination of analytical
acuity and personal experience.[15]

One of the more powerful challenges to the pristine
simplicity of the "neoclassical" school was based on revised
definitions of rationality, which led to new appreciation for
complexities of human behavior along with more predictive
empirical models. If in the traditional model rationality was
defined as the search for *optimal* courses of action given all the
necessary information from which to compare all possible options, the expanded and more realistic definition included
the notion of "bounded" rationality: because most people are
limited in their information-processing capacity, they do not
pursue optimal solutions to complex problems but rather
choose actions that are *reasonably good* based on appropriate
deliberation. Voltaire's warning to not let pursuit of perfection be the enemy of good found expression in twentieth-

century laboratories where operations researchers, cognitive psychologists, computer scientists, and economists broke out of their respective silos and worked together on new "models of man." The "new institutional economics" followed, which developed a compelling alternative to understanding and dealing with problems of industrial organization, antitrust, and contract law, and, most importantly, got transaction costs out of hiding. The romantic suggestion that agents trapped in an externality condition (think of our friends in that smoky elevator) can bargain their way out of it only works if there are no barriers to engaging in such negotiations (which Mark Twain would have surely called a "stretcher"). If markets are ubiquitous, as Oliver Williamson would frequently note, so are transaction costs that cripple the otherwise elegant expectation that competition and the price system can solve all our problems. Pioneers in this research were justly awarded Nobel prizes.[16]

Economics can be criticized for mathematical abstraction that seems to most people disconnected from practical realities, but rumors of its willful neglect and culpability in creating—rather than just chronicling and underestimating—hazards of unregulated self-interest are exaggerated. On the contrary, modifications of traditional theory have displaced the twin assumptions undergirding much of "positive" economics, namely that people have all the information they need to maximize their self-interest and that when freed to act accordingly the result will be ideal (or optimal) for society as a whole. The alternative specification, that information is rarely perfect, and that individual rational judgment may accumulate in social misfortune, is increasingly prominent in modern economics textbooks. Hayek and Friedman have their acolytes, but so do a long list of the most venerable names in the field who do not bow at the altar of market dogma. To be more specific: it's not the profession, per se, that ignores limits to free choice, even if some of its prolific contributors still lean in that direction; the bigger problem is an entire generation (or more) of policy makers and pundits for whom government, in the sadly immortal words of President Reagan, is the problem, not the solution.*

Fifty years later, principles of collective action, public goods, and externalities—staples of good graduate programs in public policy, law, and the social sciences but not yet in teacher education—are mostly inaudible in the discourse among members of Congress, some residents of the White House and many state capitols, other high officials charged with addressing our most pressing problems, and talk-show hosts with large followings. And this is in the face of all-too-familiar evidence of the effects of "government off our backs" fundamentalism. Just when we most needed energetic and judicious leadership to prevent the spread of the novel coronavirus, we mourned thousands of preventable deaths due to

---

* Game theory has, to a large extent, displaced "constrained optimization" as the staple of mathematical economics. At risk of oversimplification, the latter model was rooted in a definition of rationality that assumes individuals act as "atomistic" agents in pursuit of goals such as "utility maximization" or "cost minimization." In contrast, game theory posits rules that acknowledge interaction effects of actors involved in complex decisions, which result in different equilibrium solutions. Still, embedded in much of contemporary economic reasoning is the notion that people and organizations aspire, in one way or another, to advancing (if not "optimizing") their position. Game theory, too, is housed in a dense mathematical architecture.

anti-science rabble-rousing and ideological opposition to government intervention (much of it coming from the pinnacle of governmental power). Unwillingness to provide accurate information about origins of the disease and effectiveness of various treatments, and, as perniciously, opposition to mandates recommended by public health professionals, put America in the top ten internationally in COVID-19-related mortality. Biostatisticians at Columbia University showed "the importance of early intervention and aggressive response in controlling the COVID-19 pandemic," noting further that "[had] control measures been implemented just 1–2 weeks earlier, a substantial number of cases and deaths could have been averted." Instead, resistance to rules of social distancing and other nonpharmaceutical interventions was responsible for 650,000 unnecessary cases of infection and 35,000 unnecessary deaths. As the editor of the *New Yorker* David Remnick lamented, "How many . . . people died because they chose to believe the President's dismissive accounts of the disease rather than what public-health officials were telling the press?"[17]

Fortunately, the good sense—the good "commons sense"—of many people to abide by public health recommendations despite efforts to associate such action with weakness, or worse yet, anti-Americanism, prevented even more horrible scenarios. Equally fortunately, the allergy to political intervention did not spread to all branches of the federal government, which committed billions to support research and eventual distribution of vaccines. For yet another pleasantly surprising anomaly, congressional funding for scientific research *increased* during the Trump years. Still, the fact that vaccines were developed, tested, and delivered in record time was testament mainly to the scientific community's dogged dedication to the public good—even in the face of governmental hesitation (the initial suggestion that ingesting Clorox would do the trick was not well received)—and to mobilization of substantial capital in the private sector. Starting in January 2021, the tone and quality of presidential leadership changed, mercifully, and though debate continued about the "tyranny" of mandates and the moral superiority claimed by anti-vaxxers, the effectiveness of coherent collective action gradually became evident in the statistics of transmission, hospitalizations, and deaths. But we're nowhere near resisting the seductive lure of free enterprise. During the Omicron outbreak, a federal agency's attempt to require vaccines in private companies with 100 or more employees was quashed by the Supreme Court. A week later, a federal court judge overturned the White House plan to require federal employees to be vaccinated, and in April 2022 a federal judge lifted the requirement for masks in public transportation. Preserving business rights (and personal liberties defined in the spirit of free market behavior) won out over protecting public health.*

THE POWER OF ASSUMPTIONS . . . AND THE ASSUMPTION OF POWER

If we are to include in civic education a more full-throated decomposition of the subtleties of free choice and its conse-

---

* There are good arguments suggesting that the mask mandate, when implemented, may have been too strict and lasted too long (China's radical shutdown in 2022–23 is perhaps the most dreadful example). Still, on balance my sense is we would have been better off with at least an informed debate over the advantages and risks of government-imposed constraints on individual "rights."

quences, in hopes of implementing Adam Smith's plea for us to live together without causing one another harm, it is important to clarify underlying assumptions. The central tenet of models showing the social risks of individual acts is that the actors are basically *good people* trying to be smart and do the right thing. I distinguish here between rational or enlightened self-interest, and greed: one can apply sound principles of personal financial management while still hoping to contribute positively to the public welfare. Put differently, we know that evil lurks in the minds and hearts of some people and we accept without much argument that they need to be identified and dealt with through the justice system. Legal treatment of villains is constrained by due process and often occurs after considerable damage has been done (by the time Bernie Madoff was caught, thousands of innocent lives and livelihoods were wrecked). But who would argue against the forcefully visible hand of prosecutorial authority and the idealism of a "society of law" when it comes to preventing or addressing criminal activity designed to cause harm?

Models of individual choice and social consequences, in contrast, illuminate a different question: What happens when good people do what they think is sensible, and the result is awful and annoyingly unavoidable? Here is a simplified example drawn from the literature of environmental economics. I may correctly calculate that my exhaust-fuming jalopy makes no measurable difference to the quality of the air and that the money I'd spend on a more environmentally efficient replacement might be better targeted to buying books for poor kids. The problem is that because so many other good and smart people apply similar logic, we may all be worse off—as the polar icecaps melt and our planet gets closer to its untimely end. Moreover, whatever hopes we have about uplifting life chances of the disadvantaged might be dashed if enough people conclude that "since everyone else is buying books my efforts will be trivial." (Those kids' life expectancies may decline regardless of the books they read, because of all the pollution our jalopies cause.)

This is the essence of a logic that explains what happens in places where the majority, if polled, would express their deep concern for environmental quality: expecting people to buy more efficient cars without some sort of enforceable government intervention (or other effective collective action mechanism) is naïve. It is noteworthy that even in communities known for their love of the outdoors and the beauty of nature, say California or Montana, it takes law to get people to do what they know in their hearts is right collectively even if not individually. That begs a fundamental question: Why *require* people to do what they know and believe is morally correct? The logic is more complicated when socially good behavior is compatible with individual rationality. Borrowing from the world of automobile travel, the fact that wearing seat belts is mandated and enforced through clever incentive policies such as "click it or ticket" suggests that when left to set their own risk-benefit thresholds, well-meaning people might undermine their well-being and society's.*

---

* Without getting into all the intricacies of this example, it's worth noting that wearing seat belts contributes not only to personal health and safety but to the *social* good as well, for example by exerting downward pressure on insurance costs. In a more macabre moment in 2021, I suggested a COVID-19 variation

We may dream of a more utopian world, in which home-
owners shovel not only the snow on their front steps but also
at busy intersections where they have no property rights, and
in which people who wash their own cars also wash cars they
rent. Until such dreams become real, though, the challenge
is devising sensible policy interventions with acceptable degrees of governmental or collective coercion. Including such
concepts in civics curricula might prepare future leaders to
approach this paradox of liberty creatively and respectfully—
not exactly the adverbs that come to mind these days when
reflecting on the last few decades of congressional discourse.

A moral of this story is that we all face the dilemma of
becoming prisoners to our own rationality. The point needs
to be underscored: bad things can happen even when people
are well-informed and well intentioned. (Clearly that assumption did not characterize President Trump and his apostles,
whose disparagement of science and encouragement of socially irresponsible behavior do not qualify, in my mind at
least, as either smart or good.) But two caveats are necessary.
First, as powerful as theories of market failure are, it is wrong
to jump casually to the other extreme and rely on politics and
bureaucracy as the panacea. If markets produce untenable
inequalities and other suboptimal outcomes, so too corrective
responses can yield unintended and even possibly perverse effects. Indeed, in the light of evidence on the failure of systems such as those installed in the former Soviet Union, where
virtually all economic allocations were handled through an

---

on "click it or ticket": *mask it or casket*. (Fortunately, that did not become the
basis for a public health campaign.)

impossibly cumbersome bureaucracy of central planning, it is not surprising that calls for even marginally more muscular government regulation are met with some trepidation. The autocratic oppression in contemporary China offers perhaps the most potent warning against the temptations of centralized control, its effects on reversing poverty and raising the standard of living for millions notwithstanding. (Conservative leanings of many immigrants from communist countries are understandable.) When one considers the grievous risks of authoritarianism, the alarm bells ring ever more loudly.[18]

Second, and on a more positive note, research motivated by new theories of rationality provides relief from the depressing assumption that people always act purely in their rational self-interest without regard for the possibility that everyone might be worse off than they could be. If we accept the notion that rationality is not only "bounded" but can be "unbound" to accommodate a more socially responsible ethos, the aggregation of self-interest may not inevitably be societal calamity. Although the framers of the theory of bounded rationality did not make the explicit connection, acknowledgement of cognitive limits to rationality may lead to a more hopeful forecast of socially good acts: communitarian impulses, possibly nonrational in the sense of pure self-interest seeking, can become manifest as a personal preference for the common good.

At risk of whiplash from this circularity of logic, it is worth contemplating if altruism is how people advance their own private values or, in economics lingo, maximization of "utility." This possibility complicates the analytics but suggests—at least to a congenital optimist such as myself—that over time people become aware of the downside risks of unbridled self-interest seeking and choose to act in the public interest even if it costs them. There is evidence to support this encouraging hypothesis: more than 80 percent of polled Americans said they would be willing to pay higher prices at the gas pumps for the sake of combating Russia's demonic invasion of Ukraine. And although almost no one washes their rental cars, more people today pick up after their pets and buy relatively more expensive plant-based foods, and fewer throw trash out of their car windows or dump garbage in the corner lot than perhaps decades ago.

Let me underscore, then, that my argument about the psychological and even moral forces that favor self-interest seeking should not be taken as a denial of innately good intentions and moral rectitude of vast numbers of people. In 2020, Americans donated roughly $450 billion to charitable causes, putting us in the top twenty most generous nations of the world (yet another anomaly for a country famously but somewhat erroneously known for its individualistic "look out for yourself first" culture). The sad fact is that among elected leaders and other elites (including clergy), a relatively small number appreciate (or vocalize) the need for collective action; instead, too many of them play to their "base" and choose to perpetuate lies and misstatements—which can have frightening ripple effects on the morality of the masses. The roughly ten-year reign of Father Coughlin as the "radio priest," whose rabid pro-Nazi and Fascist rhetoric was steeped in accusations against the Jews and other enemies out to destroy our capitalist system, attracted multitudes of screaming supporters mesmerized by his demagoguery of demonization. Senator

Joseph McCarthy wrecked the lives of many people, and more recently Senator (Dr.) Rand Paul succeeded in raising money from a website that called for the removal of Dr. Anthony Fauci.[19]

FROM MODELS TO METHOD: POLITICAL ECONOMY IN CURRICULUM

If I am correct that most people, whether motivated by religious or other teaching, want to do what is right and what is good, then a task of civics and civic education—to prepare future leaders with knowledge and skill to combat the forces of ignorance that lead to autocracy and mass violence—may not be as daunting as it appears. In any case, my goal in this book is not to have civics in schools or civic education more broadly espouse a particular political stance, although I take as axiomatic the defensible democratic aspiration to egalitarian justice and pursuit of the public good. Rather it is to equip current and future leaders with knowledge of inherent paradoxes of pluralism, including legitimate disagreement over tastes and preferences and values, and give them a toolkit to help understand and manage them.

With the advent of mathematical models, we now have greater appreciation of conditions that warrant collective action of various types, along with methods to estimate their positive and negative effects both in the aggregate and as they are distributed in the population. How do these models work? Rather than attempt an exhaustive survey, I will review here the "prisoner's dilemma," high on my list of greatest hits in theories of choice and consequences. Based on my experience teaching it to graduate students some years ago, I believe it belongs in teacher education and high school classrooms, and I would add that it should work equally well in framing testimony before Congress or in presentations to corporate boards. (I will offer other examples in chapter 3.)

Here is the basic story, paraphrased from the *Stanford Encyclopedia of Philosophy*:[20]

> Michael and Richie have been arrested for robbing a bank and are placed in separate isolation cells. They are caring friends, but they both care more about maximizing their personal freedom than about the other's welfare: they are self-interest seeking in the conventional sense. The district attorney makes them each the same intriguing offer: "You may confess [cooperate with the DA] or remain silent. If you confess and your accomplice remains silent, I will drop all charges against you and use your testimony in state's evidence to ensure that your accomplice does serious time. Likewise, if your accomplice confesses while you remain silent, he will go free while you do the time. If you both confess, I get two convictions, but I'll see to it that you both get early parole. If you both remain silent, I'll have to settle for short sentences on lesser charges."

Whether variations of this game are permitted in real criminal justice systems is unclear, given that they unfairly and sneakily exploit the prisoners' natural instincts that prevent them from acting in what would be their real self-interest. To understand the logic here, a picture is helpful (and works nicely as an instructional tool). In figure 3, called a "payoff

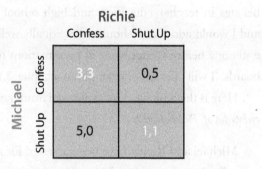

FIGURE 3. The prisoner's dilemma

matrix," numbers in the cells are years in prison (hence large numbers are bad); the first number in each pair is the payoff to Michael, the second number is the payoff to Richie.

Let's look first at the dilemma from Richie's perspective. He thinks to himself: "I don't know for sure what Michael will do, but if he confesses, I'd be better off confessing because three years in jail is better than five; and if he remains silent, I'd still be better off confessing because zero years in jail is better than one. Therefore, my dominant strategy has to be to confess." Because Michael applies the same logic, he, too, confesses.

And they both get three years behind bars when, had they both remained silent, they would have been sentenced to just one year each.

The moral of the story is about the conflict between individual and group rationality: these smart guys acted in their own best interest, and both were made worse off. It is worth recalling that in this case our two hapless prisoners have all the necessary data (perfect information) and are able to compute the payoffs to every possible course of action (they can be rational in the traditional sense). Extensions of the model to situations where those assumptions are relaxed, or to multiplayer and iterative versions, make the mathematics more complex but not much different in their basic result. It may be clear now why these games have a *tragic* quality: simple, intuitive, reasonable assumptions do not overcome the logic that leads ineluctably to failure.

Tragedy is of course not an idea unique to political economy. In history and literature, it implies human downfall or death caused by inner demons (Hamlet, Oedipus), external evil (Adolf Eichmann, Joseph Stalin), or random catastrophe (Otis Redding, Jayne Mansfield). In behavioral and social science, though, the word has special meaning. As articulated by Garrett Hardin in his famous 1968 paper, tragedy refers to situations in which instincts of self-preservation and rational use of limited resources lead to bad outcomes. Although references to the basic problem of managing common resources preceded Hardin, his article became one of the most cited in all of science. Inspired in part by his intuition that a significant class of problems (including the arms race) may have no "technical solution," he offered the parable of herdsmen wishing to keep as many cattle as possible in a pasture open to all; the simple analytics dictate that from the point of view of each herdsman, the benefit of adding cattle significantly exceeds the cost of reduction in total available grazing land. As he put it, "Therein is the tragedy. Each man is locked into a system that compels him to increase his herd without limit . . . *freedom in a commons brings ruin to all*" (italics added). It is this remorseless logic that makes the situation tragic (Hardin invokes Alfred North Whitehead's observation that "the essence of dramatic tragedy . . . resides in the solemnity of the remorseless working of things").

There is an important psychological aspect to this model. What happens when we send two conflicting messages at the same time: do the morally right thing (such as watch out for the effects of your behavior on society) and do the smart thing (don't waste your money on things that will have little impact either for yourself or for society at large)? Presenting this problem of moral choice with appreciation for the challenges inherent in the calculus of individual self-interest seeking—that is, taking account for the potential cognitive dissonance that Hardin warned about—may be more effective than simply preaching for good behavior.[21]

May I then offer a friendly amendment to Isaiah Berlin's teaching? In many situations, tragedy results from innocent "sheep" behaving in their own self-interest. It is often not the case that nasty "wolves" are responsible but rather benign and ordinary people who, whether they are aware of it or not, allow their individually rational impulses to aggregate into perplexing and frustrating suboptimal outcomes. Unfortunate things happen even as a result of actions taken by good people, a distinguishing takeaway from the commons model. But two additional caveats are necessary. First, the possibility of unwanted social consequences resulting from innocent and rational individual choice is *not* an apology for, nor a legitimization of, the abandonment of morality associated with mass hysteria and cultlike behavior leading to tyranny and political violence. On the contrary, with any lesson on, say, the prisoner's dilemma, it is essential to reaffirm the obligation of individuals to resist temptations of blindly going along with the crowd, and with that, the responsibility of society to create and sustain an environment conducive to individual moral behavior. The literature on "innocent bystanders" during the Nazi holocaust, for example, would be an appropriate complement to teaching the commons logic.

Second, although the fundamental logic in the metaphor of wolves and sheep is compelling enough to include in civic education, introducing the dilemma of unregulated individualism certainly does not mean proselytizing against freedom or denying the possibility that rational individuals can and often do make socially productive choices. This point has been substantiated in a growing literature with rigorous empirical and experimental evidence, thanks to the pathbreaking work of Elinor Ostrom and others (see box 2).

 BOX 2. UNCOMMON REBUTTALS

It may be tempting, especially for the pessimistically inclined, to infer from the model of the "tragedy of the commons" that all hope is lost, that the clash between individual self-interest and the social good must fatalistically result in dire consequences, that liberty for some means disaster for all, that a remorseless logic sentences us to the inevitable failure of free democracy. If threats from unregulated commerce and overgrazing of public resources are not worrisome enough, try Kenneth Arrow's "possibility theorem," which shows how conventional democratic voting systems are fundamentally flawed. In a word, democracy as we imagine it is complicated, if not impossible.[22]

This is an extreme version of a familiar habit among some social (and physical) scientists, who invoke the specter of "unintended consequences" to stifle debate and shake confidence in the possibility of human progress. A nefarious example was the use of such logic, spiced with a good dose of *schadenfreude*, to undermine support for public welfare. Although dismissed by serious scholars and journalists for its intentional misinterpretation of the data, the argument that federal programs make poor people poorer was just clever enough to gain political support that set back social programs by decades. When employed wisely, on the other hand, the metaphor is valid. We know, for example, that safeguards meant to guarantee resources to parents for children identified with disabilities, because of the way regulations are written and communicated, delay or deny exactly the kind of help the law was meant to provide. Acknowledging such flaws is an important step toward correcting unintended errors of implementation.

A general lesson follows. The theoretical impossibility of natural solutions to prisoner's dilemmas and other behavioral paradoxes should never be the last word. Rather, these models should be understood as inducements to reasonable people to figure out what to do even if the options are few and imperfect. They must not be seen as invitations to throw up our hands in resigned disgust with the hopeless human condition. Renowned social scientists (including three Nobelists and one who deserved to win the prize) are champions of this more enlightened approach. In one of Albert Hirschman's most compelling books, he provided a powerful antidote to the poison of policy stasis by carefully dissecting the "rhetoric of reaction" as applied by critics of the French

Revolution (especially Edmund Burke), opponents of universal suffrage, and skeptics unconvinced about the moral and economic rationale for public assistance to lift the poor. The central insight in this remarkable book is that a linchpin of rigorous policy analysis—namely, subjecting reform proposals to high evidentiary standards—can be exploited by ideologues who are determined to resist social and economic change. Although he did not directly reference the commons problem, Hirschman alerted us to the danger of treating overgrazing and other models of the social effects of individual behavior as immutable laws of nature and using them to shirk civic responsibility by cynically citing the risks, costs, and imperfections of any solution strategy.[23]

Approached from a different perspective—cognitive psychology and human information processing—Herbert Simon's argument for redefining rationality dovetails with Hirschman's cautions about the misuse of evidentiary standards. Simon's challenges to economic orthodoxy and the holy grail of optimization (for which he was awarded the Nobel Prize in 1978) provide a scientifically validated case for decisions that meet standards of *reasonableness* rather than *perfection*. History brims with abundant evidence of the bloody results of utopianism: Can civics instruction steer us in more peaceful directions? Because many interesting problems are too complex for computable optimal solutions, the question is whether to suspend rigorous judgment altogether or to acknowledge the bounds of our rationality and pursue action that is likely, at least in some predictable ways, to move in the direction of progress. In the case of the commons, do we drop the idea of collective response to reduce risks and harms of self-interest? Or do we seek consensus for strategies that reasonably mitigate—rather than optimally eliminate—unwanted outcomes? (Simon's introduction of terms such as "bounded" and "procedural" rationality changed the course of economic [and social] science. See, e.g., Simon 1976.) Can we sustain focus long enough to consider mechanisms to account for, and possibly compensate the victims of, imperfect policy responses?

With respect to the commons problem specifically, theoretical and experimental research by political scientist Elinor Ostrom (who shared the Nobel Prize in Economic Sciences in 2009 with Oliver Williamson, a protégé of Simon's), is an antidote to the inevitability of tragic outcomes. In her presidential address to the American Political Science Association in 1998, Ostrom outlined the parameters of a hopeful rebuttal to remorselessly tragic commons situations. She approached the problem with eyes wide open: "Social dilemmas occur whenever individuals in interdependent situations face choices in which the maximization of short-term self-interest yields outcomes leaving all participants worse off than feasible alternatives." But she hints early on that history may actually be on our side: "In prehistoric times, simple survival was dependent both on the aggressive pursuit of self-interest and on collective action to achieve cooperation in defense, food acquisition, and child rearing. Reciprocity among close kin was used to solve social dilemmas. . . . As human beings began to settle in communities and engage in agriculture and long-distance trade, forms of reciprocity with individuals other than close kin were essential to achieve mutual protection, to gain the benefits of long-distance trading, and to build common facilities and preserve common-pool resources."

Based on her extensive research and review of the burgeoning literature of social choice, including experiments undertaken by psychologists, evolutionary biologists, economists, and others, Ostrom cautioned vigorously against the deterministic overinterpretation of commons dilemmas. "What do these experiments tell us? . . . That individuals temporarily caught in a social-dilemma structure are likely to invest resources to innovate and change the structure itself in order to improve joint outcomes." Ostrom (1990, 1998) is unflinching in her appreciation that government is neither the only nor the most reliable solution, and that the subtleties of devising arrangements that preserve freedom while protecting the public good should be priorities for civic education. It will not surprise readers of this book that I would have liked to be present during Ostrom's presidential address and applaud her parting message: "For those who wish the twenty-first century to be one of peace, we need to translate our research findings on collective action into materials written for high school and undergraduate students." Amen.*

---

* It warms my heart to think that a beloved mentor, Oliver Williamson, of blessed memory, shared the Nobel stage with Ostrom, whom I never met.

In the light both of the seemingly inevitably tragic aspects of commons behavior and the evidence that societies actually find ways, naturally and/or with the help of a visible governmental or other coercive hand, to avoid the direst consequences of individual choice, the curricular challenges are real. The goal should be equipping people living in democratic pluralist societies with an analytical framework that allows them to consider conditions under which the commons logic prevails, conditions favoring individual choices that defy that logic, and, perhaps most important, ways in which modern societies can devise arrangements to reduce or eliminate the downside risks of unregulated "grazing" without succumbing to the temptations of totalitarianism. (Hardin's words were used to justify repressive population control policies and other dictatorial interventions that would, thankfully, be anathema in the United States and most industrialized democracies.)

To unpack this argument—that the solution to commons dilemmas is not necessarily to rely exclusively on unregulated bargaining or the overwrought imposition of government edicts—requires attention both to the range of situations for which it is relevant and to the idea that creative policy analysis offers options with advantages and disadvantages. Scholars of political economy should not be the sole proprietors of this approach to comparative institutional analysis, and of the models that shed light on alternative strategies to manage tensions between individual freedom and the civic good. The ideas need to become staples of civic reasoning in and out of schools.

One more example of the basic theoretical proposition concerning choice and consequences helps to set the stage for development of enriched civics curricula. If cattle-grazing is not the best metaphor to engage young people (of all ages) in the paradoxes of liberalism, the crisis of climate change might resonate more forcefully. Assuming that global warming is caused largely by consumption of fossil fuels (now the consensus of the overwhelming majority of scientists), the question is whether the commons logic helps explain why it so difficult to find and implement corrective strategies. Again, one need not incorporate the views of malevolent climate change deniers for whom the evidence of impending global catastrophe is all part of a conspiratorial hoax; let's focus instead on the good intentions of the majority and consider why those intentions continue to pave a road to disaster.

For economists and other students of externalities, the global climate problem is a familiar, albeit magnified, case of individual (or localized) rationality colliding with the best interests of the planet. The analytics, again, are remorseless: as suggested by the example of holding on to an environmentally unsound car, pollution of air (and other natural resources) can be modeled in terms of the way individuals or, in this case, nations "do the math." No single person's morally upstanding refusal to dump effluents into the neighboring stream is going to make a measurable difference on water quality generally, unless of course everyone chooses the socially responsible option. In that case, say rational thinkers to themselves, if everyone is doing it I can save the cost of going to the recycling plant and it will hardly matter. And there is the psychological problem that Hardin noted, when we send two conflicting messages: do the morally right thing (don't pollute) and do the smart thing (don't waste your money). Creating opportunities for cognitive dissonance ought not be a goal or outcome of public policy.

The conundrum applies globally. Which nation wants to carry more than its fair share of the total burden? Granted, it is reassuring to live in a society governed by people with a public conscience who make geopolitical decisions based not solely on calculations of national (self) interest defined only in the seemingly cold language of economic benefit and cost. A good example: to our great good fortune, we could have saved large sums of money by waiting even longer before going to war against the Nazis and fascists, but thankfully a moral imperative ultimately prevailed. At the same time, whether it is reasonable to expect the United States to solve the climate problem without assurance that other polluters are participating eludes the cognitive dissonance problem. Rational leaders in all countries face the dilemma, as none of them wants to be paying the costs so that others "ride free." We are all caught in a frightful stalemate and must weather (!) the angry recriminations of those—especially in the generation that will inherit our environmental mess—who are fed up with our inability to fix things.[24]

Describing the commons problem is necessary but insufficient if our goal is to provide decision makers with more confidence to devise creative remedies. As I will argue in chapter 3, the challenging educational task is translating some of the best models from political economy into practical and relevant examples for teacher-educators, high school students, and the broader public. To set the stage for this discussion, the next chapter reviews the current and historical status of civics education, necessary to contemplate where and how principles of collective action might find a place.

CIVICS AS PROCESS AND PRODUCT

ORIGINS AND OPPORTUNITIES

I insist that the object of all true education
is not to make men carpenters, it is to make
carpenters men.

W. E. B. Du Bois

The people who live in a golden age usually
go around complaining how yellow everything looks.

Randall Jarrell

WITH SO MUCH PUBLIC and professional interest in revived civics education, it may be tempting to pine for the days when
concepts of social responsibility, political participation, community engagement, and the public welfare had a formal and

stable presence in K–12 pedagogy and young people were getting what they needed to be functional democratic citizens. After all, "revival" suggests restarting and reenergizing something good. Simple arithmetic suggests a more complicated situation. Let's not forget that many of today's most strident politicians—including perpetrators of political mischief, conspiracy-mongering, hate speech, narcissistic authoritarianism, and racism—were in high school in the 1950s and 1960s, when we'd like to think education (and much else) was in a golden age. On the other hand, and with apologies again for my perhaps irrational optimism, a sizable majority of today's leaders in business, science, teaching, and the arts came through our inchoate K–12 system with a passion for sustaining and fulfilling our founding egalitarian principles and working for the collective good. If this more hopeful view of things suggests we need not worry about—and spend money on—civic education, that is not the intent. On the contrary, I hope that with a revived and intensified effort involving schools and their external environment, a larger and more sustained majority of our population will choose—and become—leaders capable of judicious and balanced decision making.

Which begs a fundamental question: if our schools accept their significant but limited role in the national course correction needed to protect democracy, where and how will the relevant skills and knowledge be taught? My hope is to infuse in high school teaching and learning, via enriched teacher education programs in colleges and universities, lessons from a specific body of thought, what I have been calling "political economy" as shorthand for collective action and finding balance between private and public provision of fundamental social goods, it is important to consider if the host body will be hospitable to such a transplant. Where were—are—these issues covered (if at all)? What skills and behaviors are included, explicitly or implicitly, under that rubric? Is there room for more?

To address those questions, I begin this chapter with a review of the origins of civics and meanings of "the civic good" in American education, and move then into a more detailed discussion of the current situation as manifest in the complex web of federal, state, and local standards. I will refer to the swings in educational history between a focus on the political and moral goals of schooling and its more economic or "human capital" and skills-development purposes. And I will refer to the peculiarly American tension between the preference for limited centralized governmental involvement in the content of schooling, on the one hand, and the recurrent sense that there is a legitimate political role for articulation of expectations regarding the values that schools are supposed to inculcate in youth. That seesaw has rarely found a stable equilibrium, and indeed, today we are again experiencing painful ups and downs, especially as awareness of racial and economic injustices engenders debates about the foundational purposes of public schooling, what to include and exclude from our history and literature, and more broadly the definitions of phrases such as "American values."

At the risk of simplification of the more complicated history and its effects on the changing ecology of curriculum, my reading of the data suggests that ideals of self-governance, the rule of law, the workings of a complex market-based economy, and the pursuit of freedom and justice were rarely, if ever, organized into a coherent "civics" pedagogy. They were, and to a large extent still are, scattered across programs in history, government, the social studies, geography, economics, literature, and, yes, even the physical and natural sciences. As historian Jill Lepore (2022) noted regarding an early twentieth-century textbook, "*A Civic Biology* [was] more than a guide to life on earth . . . [it] was a *civics primer*, a guide to living in a democracy" (italics added). The diffusion of concepts of citizenship across so many traditional areas means, on the one hand, that they must have been considered high on the list of valued purposes of schooling—a good thing—even if they were not afforded their own coherent curriculum. On the other hand, it means that even under the best of circumstances, resuscitating civics in today's already congested high school schedule will be more complicated than dusting off old syllabi and transferring them from mimeographed sheets to electronic slideshows.

Before we dig into complexities of curriculum development, it is worth recalling a familiar story about why any of this matters. Upon exiting the Constitutional Convention in 1787, Benjamin Franklin was asked what sort of government the delegates had created—a republic or a monarchy. His answer: "A republic, if you can keep it." Franklin, along with Jefferson and Madison and other founders understood the fragility of their invention, and they thought education was perhaps the most promising preservative. In the words of the eminent political scientist Lorraine McDonnell (2000), "The original rationale for public schooling in the United

States was the preparation of democratic citizens who could preserve individual freedom and engage in responsible self-government."

But the details of what children in school should be taught were left murky. Instead, in the ensuing decades (and centuries), the implicit model relied on the aspiration to develop in young people a civic *orientation* rather than attempt a formulaic definition of everything that intuitively appealing notion might embody. American schools took on the challenge with a characteristic blend of exceptionalism and selective policy borrowing. The particular ways in which the content and form of civic education were negotiated, along with many other aspects of public schooling, reflected subtleties and complexities of our evolving social and political environment and, clearly, a rejection of most things that smacked of old-world statism. As the intellectual historian Paul Mendes-Flohr put it, "The American experiment began by throwing out Europe's blueprints." On the other hand, the American system, which was so deeply rooted in revolutionary concepts at the core of our independence, shared at arm's length the approach to developing civic knowledge in Britain, where "[school-based] citizenship education was suspected of being indoctrinating." Similarly, in another example of policy-borrowing, nineteenth-century education reformers imported the idea of compulsory schooling from Prussia—coating it as always with a distinctive American veneer.

This reticence to allow the federal government to weigh in on matters of curriculum content is evidence of a more general tendency in American political culture to sidestep—at least at the national level—questions most fraught with ideology or religion, as a way to avoid controversies that might have pulled threads out of the fragile republican tapestry while it was still on the loom. Compromises to save the nascent union abounded and were manifest in education as well. Separating national government from the inner workings of schools reflected a belief that some decisions, such as exactly what to teach children, may better be left in the hands and minds of families and communities and shielded from the clumsy claws of central government. As the political philosopher Michael Walzer noted, "Civil society . . . would include a great variety of ethnic and religious and perhaps even racial groups, but the members of these groups would acquire the 'inestimable' good of citizenship only after a long period of practical education . . . in democratic virtue. Meanwhile, their children would get a formal education." But what exactly to include in that formal education was not viewed as a task the federal government was equipped to take on. Philosophical and political preferences—in particular an ideological allergy to centralized authority—were reinforced by an awareness, perhaps unstated but surely appreciated at least tacitly, of the practical limits to big government bureaucracy.[1]

That combination of ideology and practicality, integral to American "pragmatism," shaped the development of public education for the long term. Fast-forward to the present, and it is instructive to compare our quite intentionally dispersed system to, say, the more orderly situation in France, where curriculum decisions are almost all handled by the central ministry. It might be tempting to attribute the difference to size; after all, today the population of France is about one-fifth that of the United States. But even in states with smaller populations than that of France (e.g., California with 39 million, Texas with 30 million) authority is diffused across multiple districts. Florida, population 22 million, has roughly 75 independent districts. Although state boards of education and governors in those places are increasingly willing to impose political ideologies on curriculum planning and instruction, their authority is circumscribed by the culture of local control that has long and entangled roots.

Taking this logic one step further, although the American education system (or what James Conant called our education chaos) is often criticized for its stodginess, there is a good argument to be made for the advantages of localized agility that promotes experimentation and change. Of course, too much of that may not be a good thing either: as the late Richard Elmore once noted, in commenting on the slow pace of reform and the burdens placed on teachers and administrators to try all kinds of novel ideas that had not yet been tested theoretically or empirically, "Our schools are awash in innovation." Where to set the dial between local and national control, between the *pluribus* and the *unum*, is one way to encapsulate two centuries of debate over school policy. Reform proposals, therefore, about education generally and the meanings of civics specifically will have to confront the preference for diffused governance and associated suspicions about governmental overreach. Pursuit of optimal—rather than reasonably good—solutions under these circumstances does not seem like the rational approach.[2]

Although the word "pragmatism" is the subject of scholarship and theorizing in political science and philosophy, a simplified definition that works well for my purposes focuses on society's willingness to accept compromise, ambiguity, and reasonableness rather than to hold out for perfect solutions and utopian fantasies. It ties to what Albert Hirschman meant by "possibilism." Note, however, that tolerance of some vagueness in such matters as what moral principles and ethical values young people should acquire is not to be confused with apathy or silence about what should be taught. On the contrary, American society has always thrived on robust argumentation: even as we acknowledged, implicitly, the cognitive and political bounds to specifying a formula for civics instruction, we never stopped debating what the concept meant and how to teach it. And elected officials at all government levels have always attempted to voice their position on these murky issues, with varying degrees of fervency. Clearly, the third decade of this century is one that so far seems especially fraught with political and partisan bickering over core values.

The policy and practical debates are partly definitional and partly situational. For example, as suggested by McDonnell and echoed in the writings of other political scientists, civics education was meant to deal "primarily with the relationship of the person to the state." Others, though, preferred to focus on notions of moral discipline—that is, teaching young people the things they need to know in order to behave responsibly in their personal and community lives. Still others, though interestingly in the minority at least until relatively recently, wanted young people to learn the workings of the economy, which arguably would make a difference in the ways they managed their personal finances and family budgets. Imagine what it would take to establish a viable consensus among these compelling definitions and competing intellectual traditions, and turn it into a curriculum that would not gobble every minute of every school day!

Indeed, the time constraint is key to understanding the situational or practical challenge. Assuming a compromise can be reached among diverse interests and preferences for what civics means, which may seem naïve in the light of what we know about the fragility of consensus-seeking processes, the next step is finding room for it in a crowded system striving to provide young people with vocational skills, general literacy, and management of personal life. As education historian Fred Newman put it, in that "supermarket" conception of curriculum, "Our troubles are due in part to . . . the lack of a coherent conception of education for civic competence." However, if the conception is incoherent, or perhaps more charitably, democratically pluralist, it's not for lack of trying. The major turning points in educators' understandings and preferences for what to teach and how were stimulated by changing attitudes to the political and social context and shaped by stark differences in underlying philosophies of education. To stretch the metaphor, the aisles in that crowded supermarket underwent periodic reshelving and relabeling, even if the end result was not necessarily a better quality of groceries.[3]

At risk of collapsing a complicated history into a few paragraphs, the shifting philosophical foundations upon which educators defined and then implemented principles of civics, starting at the turn of the twentieth century, are worth summarizing. Notably, the introduction and elaboration of what became known as "community civics" were the hall-marks of efforts by the National Education Association, culminating in a 1916 report that was viewed as "the most important document in the long history of citizenship education [which] legitimated the term 'social studies' to designate formal citizenship education and placed squarely in the field all of those subjects that were believed to contribute to that end." (Today the word "citizenship" evokes uncomfortable questions about the rights and responsibilities of immigrants and other newcomers, and is therefore less popular in the professional world of education than "civics.") As powerful as the messages in that report were, though, implementation was uneven and, for some educators, inadequate. A prominent reformer "complained in 1921 that progressive administrators and teachers were 'impatient with the further perpetuation of non-essential material in our public-school courses.'"[4]

Moving forward, in a system that has mistakenly been accused of being cemented in antiquated norms, educators in the 1950s (and then more forcefully in the 1960s in response to Russia's successful launch of Sputnik) developed what became known as the "new social studies," a movement whose motivations may seem familiar in today's turbulent environment. The existing (progressive) framework of social studies education "came under attack from both citizens and the government for the failure to promote citizenship. Events both at home and abroad eventually led to a collective reexamination of the overall purpose and goals of social studies." The changes were fueled by survey data showing, inter alia, that "only 35 percent of the nation's youth believed newspapers should be allowed to print anything they want, only 34 percent believed the government should prohibit people from making speeches, only 26 percent believed that police should be allowed to search a person's home without a warrant, and only 25 percent believed that some groups should not be allowed to hold public meetings."[5]

By 1994, the zeitgeist had again spurred changes in the ways social studies educators defined their mission and specified what should be included in the curriculum. Under the aegis of the National Council for the Social Studies (NCSS), a set of curriculum standards was built on a familiar motif: "The United States and its democracy are constantly evolving and in continuous need of citizens who can adapt its enduring traditions and values to meet changing circumstances. Meeting that need is the mission of the social studies . . . [aimed at developing in students] a core of basic knowledge and ways of thinking drawn from many academic disciplines, learning how to analyze their own and others' opinions on important issues, and becoming motivated to participate in civic and community life as active, informed citizens."

The NCSS emphasized an emerging distinction familiar in today's education policy discourse: "The standards . . . define what students . . . should know and when they should know it," but they were not meant as precise curricula or syllabi. Rather, standards address overall curriculum goals and student performance expectations, while the individual disciplines (civics and government, economics, geography, history, the sciences) provide focused and enhanced content detail. The most recent revision to the standards, in 2010, updated the 1994 edition while keeping the original rubrics: culture; time, continuity, and change; people, places, and environments; individual development and identity; individuals, groups, and institutions; power, authority, and governance; production, distribution, and consumption; science, technology and society; global connections; and civic ideals and practices. Current moves to intensify civics education, such as the College, Career, and Civic Life (C3) program, build on and extend concepts in the NCSS standards.[6]

To summarize, then, the American approach to civics education has been to orient youth toward a set of norms, values, dispositions, and behaviors, buttressed with an abridged set of facts about our history and culture and political machinery. The implementation strategy, implicit in how schools were organized and in curricula and instructional methods used, but also articulated by educators, political leaders, and philosophers of education, was based on the proposition that the complexities of civics required importation of knowledge and specific analytical skills from the component academic disciplines. But writing the formula for blending those ingredients was apparently a job left to curriculum designers and teacher educators.*

Adding to these subtleties of diffused decision-making, it is important to emphasize again that civics education always included an action side: didactic methods and book learning

---

* To "orient" youth toward civic awareness and understanding of the workings of democracy means not necessarily prescribing all the detail. It's a delicate balance: by analogy, consider the difference between the decision to "head north" on a family vacation and specifying in advance whether that includes Buffalo or Boston or both. The former may be Mom and Dad's orienting prerogative, while the latter might trigger debate among the siblings.

alone were perhaps necessary, but considered insufficient if
not complemented by thoughtful and structured *experiential*
learning. In other words, navigating in this murky and con-
tested territory of values and behavior is a matter of process
(what goes on in school, who participates, who pays for it, and
how it intersects with "life on the outside") and product
(knowledge and skills that are taught formally because they
are not likely to be learned otherwise). Here process means
experience inside and outside the formal classroom environment, while product is intended to capture factual knowledge
and taught analytical skills. The meaning of that dichotomy
is different in the NCSS standards, where processes denote
what learners should be able to do (and not just what they
should know), and products are meant as tangible evidence
of learners' skills. The 1994 NCSS standards talked about
"performance expectations," which then became "processes"
in the 2010 revision. For example, a product of high school
social studies related to the theme of "culture" is "interview-
ing members of a sub-culture to which they have access (e.g.,
student sub-groups, workplace groups, or community groups)
to present the group's point of view on an issue of importance
in an editorial to the local newspaper."[7]

HOW ARE WE DOING?

The balance between product and process, between formal,
tacit, and experiential modes of teaching and learning, and
how content is distributed across the core subjects, has evolved
through history and is again in transition under intense public and professional scrutiny. An underlying assumption wo-
ven through these debates is that civic knowledge acquired in

school is valuable in its own right, and perhaps even more so if (as hoped) it translates to civic behavior. Which leads to a perhaps obvious question, especially if investments in revived curricula and instruction are to add value and if curriculum designers are going to be held accountable for measurable gains in student learning and subsequent behavior. What is the baseline from which to assess progress? How much or little do Americans actually know about the workings of their democracy? (If the answer is "enough," then my advocacy for curricular intervention will face yet another logical challenge.) I turn now to a brief overview of the current state of knowledge about . . . the state of civic knowledge. (Spoiler alert: the situation is not as bad as some headlines suggest, though there is plenty of room for improvement.)

The general consensus for some time has been that too many American students (and adults, for that matter) are woefully ignorant of the fundamental facts and tenets of their democracy. Some humility is in order, though, when issuing such grand indictments. The eminent historian Lawrence Cremin recounted, with a hint of sarcastic pleasure, an embarrassing episode. When the head of National Geographic was waxing ruefully about dreadful gaps in geographic knowledge among high school kids, he was asked by a feisty journalist (most likely educated in a public school that encouraged feisty argumentation) to name the states that border Texas. He was stumped, and the audience squirmed as they would if a child missed some notes in a youth piano recital.

Quaint anecdotes and *schadenfreude* aside, the quantitative data are not exactly a solid basis for complacency. Findings from reputable surveys such as the National Assessment of Educational Progress (NAEP) are complicated. On average, eighth graders performed a few points lower in 2022 than in 2018, returning to their place as recorded in 1998. The relationship of their factual knowledge to their sense of engagement in democratic processes suggests that good instruction can make a difference: "higher-performing students see themselves able to make a difference in their community and believe their civics schoolwork helps them understand what is happening in the world."*

NAEP data reinforce what is clearly a more urgent matter, namely persistent disparities of resources—which plays a significant role in explaining observed test-score differences—that correlate with the uneven distribution of students in proficiency brackets. Roughly 30 percent of white students but only 10 percent of Black and 12 percent of Hispanic students performed "at or above proficient" on the 2022 Assessment. International data from assessments designed and conducted by the International Association for the Evaluation of Educational Achievement (IEA) provide additional nuance and some hope: on questions about economics and inequality, for example, American 14-year-olds in 1999 scored highest among 28 participating countries, and their average performance regarding general "civic knowledge" was significantly above the mean.[8]

---

* It is not clear how students in other countries would do on similar queries of their civics facts, nor whether answering those kinds of test items is as good an indicator as observing, for example, how people actually translate their knowledge to behavior (one wonders what percentage of the Hitler Youth were well versed in theories of democracy and human rights).

Efforts by NAEP, IEA, and other large-scale assessment programs to approximate the sources and implications of proficiency in civics and other subjects, and to provide a framework for consideration of curricular and instructional reforms, are limited by complexities of measurement, meaning, and use. The lack of a consensus about exactly how to define "civic knowledge" means that all such assessments will be criticized for their emphasis on some and not other components falling under that rubric. As measurement experts know, grappling with and defining underlying constructs ideally should precede and inform the drafting and fielding of items intended to yield reliable approximations and, more importantly, valid inferences about what those approximations mean. NAEP and IEA undertake complicated (and costly) engagement with stakeholders possessing diverse views on what matters most in young persons' grasp of issues ranging from government functions to workings of the economy to notions of social cohesion and responsibility. But such findings should be viewed as estimates, rather than as measures suggestive of a chimerical degree of precision, and there will always be disagreement about what to make of the data. Political scientists, for example, are most interested in measures of knowledge of government, while other educators and social scientists may be more interested in students' grasp of economic principles, capacity to lead a moral life, or ability to work in multicultural settings as the most valued outcomes of education. It is not hard to see why developing and implementing a useful and comprehensive system to measure student learning and monitor national progress is so challenging.[9]

A second and equally daunting complexity in this work centers on the lack of conclusive evidence about the effects of school compared to environmental and home-background variables in explaining variance in whatever outcome measures are used. At a more granular level, relative effects of classroom instruction, focused vs. diffused approaches to curricula, and the uses of assessment are not what might be called "settled science." Familiar rhetoric pins the blame for alleged deficits of general civic knowledge in the population on the failure of schools, while other critiques shift attention from teachers to the confused system they must work in—namely, one which lacks national standards and admits into the teaching workforce people who have not had adequate preservice preparation. Scholars who have surveyed the relevant discourse offer important nuance: "The literature—at least about political knowledge—is neither as one-sided nor as conclusive as these views would suggest." Similarly, the relationship between formal civics instruction—whether or not it is treated as separable from history, government, and the social studies—and student proficiency on a range of measurable outcomes, is ambiguous, as are the effects of measurable differences in teacher qualifications and experience. The 1998 NAEP civics exam, for example, which focused heavily on the social studies, showed modest effects of teacher professional development and tenure in the classroom on learning outcomes. In 2022, "students whose teachers reported having primary responsibility for teaching civics . . . had a higher civics score on average . . . than students whose teachers did not indicate having primary responsibility for teaching civics." Where these diverse appraisals of the condition of civic knowledge—and how to improve it—often converge is on the role of assessment: to the extent that what teachers teach and what students learn is influenced, for better or worse, by external exams, it is understandable why nearly every discussion about reform veers into arguments over incentive (and disincentive) effects of high-stakes tests that compromise the validity of inferences based on the scores.[10]

My goal here is not to adjudicate the debate about how much our students (and the general population) know. I am willing to proceed on the assumption that no matter how well or poorly we are doing now, we could do better. (I am only half-comforted by the finding that roughly half of all Americans can name all three branches of government.) Which brings me back to the original question, regarding the proper balance between tacit (experiential) and formal (curricularized) approaches to civics teaching and learning. The first thing to acknowledge is a perhaps obvious distinction between topics included in core subjects (e.g., science, reading, and mathematics) and topics or concepts generally categorized under the rubric of civics, such as social responsibility, political knowledge and engagement, history, and moral behavior. As explained eloquently by Niemi and Junn, "It is difficult to visualize students doing word problems or reading chemistry texts on their own—and few of us would want our children experimenting in our kitchens . . . [but] in the case of civics . . . the matter is not so simple. Government and politics affect our daily lives in innumerable ways." And, I would add, many parents like to see their kids involved in their communities and in some form of political or social action. In other words, although it is impossible to calculate the precise coefficients, it is clear that some part of what students know about civics—as estimated by various standardized instruments—derives from their lived experiences, another part comes from the formal instruction they get in school, and very likely a substantial part comes from some combination.

A good example of where didactic and experiential streams cross is Problems of Democracy (POD), a popular course that was recommended in the 1916 NEA report and gained increasing interest by midcentury. Typically its purpose was to instill a greater appreciation for the complications—and virtues—of our political system. It became especially relevant during the civil rights, anti–Vietnam War, and revived women's movements of the 1960s—tumultuous real-world arenas of public engagement and political participation. POD was not in a separable civics curriculum but rather more loosely offered as an elective, usually in honors or Advanced Placement (AP) programs in history or government. An early prototype of experiential learning, this course and similar ones relied on students' day-to-day activities as source material for classroom debate on such issues as civil disobedience, majority rule, and constitutionally protected forms of protest. Simply put, what we learned in the streets we imported to our schoolrooms, and good teachers knew how to engage us in discussions by tying events taking place outside to abstract theoretical notions of politics and social justice. And the syllabus did not need to press heavily and explicitly on values, morals, and the meanings of civic responsibility; displaying a poster of Abraham Lincoln with the admonition that "to sin

by silence when they should protest makes cowards of men"
was sufficiently stimulating for most of us.[11]

There is a paradox, however, on the connection between
tacit and formal learning. As poignantly reported by the distinguished scholar of multicultural education James Banks,
based on his experience growing up in segregated Mari-
anna, Arkansas, in the 1950s, teachers' efforts to instruct
Black children about the niceties of democracy had to con-
tend with a backdrop of starkly incongruous external conditions: "The democratic ideals taught in citizenship lessons
[were] contradicted by [the day-to-day realities of] . . . racism,
sexism, social-class stratification, and inequality." In other
words, if my POD lessons circa 1968 were motivated and reinforced by data from outside our schoolhouse, in Banks's case
he had to cope with significant cognitive dissonance in recon-
ciling contradictory messages coming from lived experience
in and out of the classroom. He called that "the citizenship
education dilemma," which is fundamental to appreciating
why even the intuitively appealing notion of blended experiential and formal learning—especially of something as complicated as civics—requires attention to context. How students, especially at an early age, navigate the chasm between
what they hear in class and what they see and feel outside is
not obvious, nor is the set of skills needed by teachers who
regularly confront the challenges of knowing how—and how
much—to integrate ideology, politics, and individual preferences into their instruction and whether to allow experiences
and budding ideological dispositions among their students
(and their families) to drive classroom discussion.[12]

BOX 3. A TEACHER REFLECTS

Can/should young, preservice teachers be introduced to the idea that there is some level of acceptable personal ideology to bring into the classroom? Consider the words of a practicing educator:

> I think this is what gets teachers in trouble the most right now, because when teachers interject their personal ideologies, deliberately, without creating space for burgeoning ideologies and critical thinking of their students, these teachers can become quite vulnerable. . . . Throughout my career, there was no limit of things/ideas/topics that students threw out for discussion in my classroom, and much of it drew from the rhetoric/dialogue of their parents/ households/churches/communities. . . .
>
> How could I, as their teacher, enable these students to open their minds and make space for considering or even acknowledging opposing viewpoints from their immediate and most trusted inner circles? I don't know that in over twelve years in the classroom I ever landed on a solid answer to this question.
>
> What I do know for sure is that our students crave guidance: they need and want help to make sense of the world around them, of what their parents, their influencers, their friends, their most and least favorite teachers are saying to them.
>
> For me the puzzle was always gauging how to provoke and inspire critical thinking in such charged

environments. Pausing for thoughtful reflection (particularly in this age of social media–inspired instant gratification) may mean responding to student inquiries or quips with a "tactical" pause along the lines of "That's a great thought/idea/question . . . let me look into it and get back to you tomorrow." Which of course then requires the teacher to take the time to dig into the student comment and respond. In any case, we owe it as a form of respect to our students— and our profession—to do more than just react. Our students get enough of that outside the classroom.

Note: I am grateful to my remarkable research assistant (and GW doctoral candidate), Amanda Baker, for offering this reflection based on her experience as a high school civics teacher.

The idea of civics as process and product is not new. From the early days of the republic, the founders looked to schools as a bastion to protect the new nation from the evils of European autocracy and ensure that "we the people" would become more than just a nice turn of phrase. From the onset, there was emphasis on process—by attending school, children would become morally disciplined and ready to participate in our dynamic pluralist democracy—but as argued earlier, there was less specificity about exactly what needed to be taught and how. Political scientists Jennifer Hochschild and Nathan Scovronick offered this summary of the challenge faced by educators and curriculum developers: "The practice of democracy presumes a degree of civility, shared knowledge, the ability to communicate beyond face-to-face encounters, a willingness to play in accord with the rules of the voting game, tolerance or even respect for disparate views, equal opportunity to attain full citizenship, a common culture, and commitment to the polity even if one's electoral choice loses." It should be obvious that there could never be a simple formula to translate those noble goals into curricular checklists. Beyond the "three Rs," the necessary knowledge and skills needed to form functionally democratic citizens remained at least somewhat vague—though it certainly entailed a blend of didactic and experiential learning.[13]

FROM PROCESS TO PRODUCT?

Politics and culture shape public education in every society. In the American case, the persistent tension over jurisdictional authority for policy and practice has been a powerful determinant of the intent, implementation, and measured effectiveness of reform. At the level of policy, interventions from the mid-nineteenth century (even at the state level) to the most recent revisions to elementary and secondary legislation have focused on access, opportunity, equity, and resources. Questions of curricula were mostly viewed as off-limits, and, indeed, a good way to scare a large portion of the general population has always been to accuse reformers of sneakily trying to institute a national curriculum or national test. During the last (and somewhat tumultuous) years of the Clinton administration, circa 1998, the proposal to develop a "voluntary national test" met with fierce resistance, captured in the wry observation of a well-known education policy wonk: "Half the country hates the word 'test' and the other half hates the word 'national.'" Policy makers and members of myriad professional societies have often learned the hard way that if they dip their oars into the choppy waters of history and literature (and even scientific subjects such as evolution and climate change), their canoes will likely capsize.*

Thus, for reasons largely having to do with the ideological origins of local control trumping central government and with obstacles preventing consensus on anything but the basics, the result is that, on the whole, education leaders have traditionally been concerned with getting more kids enrolled and less so with exactly what and how they would be taught when they got there. Borrowing retrospectively from twentieth-century stand-up comedy, it was as if progressives such as Horace Mann and other "common school" reformers were motivated by the quip that "the food is terrible . . . and the portions are too small."†

Was this focus on expansion of the franchise, even with its internal imperfections, a reflection of the exceptionalist American creed that teaching values was the province of parents and not of the state, that the latter should limit its reach to providing data on student learning of material everyone more or less agreed about, and that the proper role of government was to make sure as many children as possible could benefit? It is no wonder that even as we became increasingly fascinated by the idea (and ideals) of standardized testing,

---

* I believe the quip was from Checker Finn, a prominent voice on the conservative wing of education politics. The blowup over the new Advanced Placement American history framework was a painful reminder that politics and education sometimes don't mix. See Thorp 2023b.

† Long a staple of borscht belt humor, the joke seems to have originated in a cartoon caption by Harry Hershfield in 1927.

national norms for academic performance were limited to so-called basic skills. Later attempts to include indicators of historical or literary knowledge quickly provoked resistance on partisan and ideological grounds. On the other hand, expanding the franchise and ensuring greater opportunity for the increasingly diverse demographic mosaic was viewed, with cautions and guardrails, as an acceptable area for government intervention (most recent presidents of the United States, with the possible exception of Donald Trump, declared their wish to be known as "the education president" even if resources to fuel that grand vision were never adequate). Again, beyond the basics, which everyone sensed were important for adult functioning, things as complex as "civics" were treated tacitly, more as a process than a product of schooling.

Put differently, the phrase "democratic education" has come to mean that schools can help prepare young people for democracy *by being democratic places*. As philosopher Phillip Kitcher notes, "In fostering tendencies to engage with others and to contribute to their lives, we would also induce the capacities for good citizenship. Dewey's famous linkage of democracy and education is neither arbitrary nor a penchant for teaching what he called (disdainfully) 'the civics.' Democracy, he says, is a way of life, a condition in which citizens seek to understand, and to learn from, the perspectives and the life experiences of their fellows." As artfully explained in the *Stanford Encyclopedia of Philosophy*, "Nowhere is there a better site for political or democratic action than the school itself, the students' own community. This is Dewey's insight (1916). Creating a democratic culture within the schools not only facilitates preparing students for democratic participation in the political system, but it also fosters a democratic environment that shapes the relationships with adults and among peers that the students already engage in."[14]

When did acceptance of civics as a process of schooling and byproduct of the social studies (and other subjects) evolve into calls for greater formalism in content and pedagogy? It is hard to pinpoint the exact timing and sequential relationship to other trends in school reform, but today's pressures for change have roots at least as far back as the 1960s. In the wake of what is still considered one of the most significant empirical studies of American education, the Coleman Report, which for the first time produced correlational evidence of the sources of variance in educational outcomes (mostly measured by test scores), education policy began a sustained shift from its historical emphasis on process variables (such as access, maintenance of school buildings, and allocation of financial resources) toward estimates of the productivity of schools in forming students with measurable gains in knowledge and skills. The extent to which the outcomes as estimated were attributable to school and home variables became the focus of protracted debate, which has not subsided.

In any case, the point is that disparities in school resources (inputs) were viewed by researchers and policy makers as insufficient without linking those resources to valued products of schooling. Economists later borrowed from theories of behavior of firms in competitive economies and introduced a "production function" logic to education research. In the classic formulation, achievement as measured by test scores was modeled as a function of individual student, family, school, and other "input" variables. With this increased focus on results, attention to metrics by which to gauge academic progress was a natural next step. Development of the NAEP starting roughly in 1965, which later became known as "the Nation's Report Card," was spurred by the frustration felt among senior policy officials that although states and districts were collecting data on student achievement, it was difficult to know how the nation was doing overall or how to compare different assessments used by states and districts. Estimates of average performance were not sufficient without attention to geographical variation and disparities between minority and disadvantaged students compared to their white majority peers.[15]

Measured outcomes in the early days of NAEP emphasized mathematics and reading, and complemented emerging international large-scale assessments (ILSA) of achievement between the United States and our global economic competitors. The first effort to compare American youth to peers in a selected set of industrialized countries, circa 1964, produced alarming news: the United States ranked at the bottom in mathematics. Here was another opportunity for rational deliberation that unfortunately got stifled by policy makers, advocates, and even accomplished researchers grabbing for partisan political advantage. This venture into global comparability, embraced to this day by educators eager to learn from colleagues and competitors overseas, coincided with changing attitudes and evolving economic contexts of public education. Historian Carl Kaestle, in his essay on "the political economy of citizenship," discussed the trend as it related to the nation's growth as an industrialized world power: "At a surface level there does appear to have been a shift from the eighteenth- and nineteenth-century emphasis on the political functions of schools to a post–World War II emphasis on the economic functions of schools, and that indeed the economic functions have become more salient and more consequential in the past fifty years." Kaestle noted, however, that "the earlier ideas about the functions of schools were not simply political but rather were based on a notion of the political economy of the country, whether an agrarian republic in the case of Jefferson or an industrial democracy in the eyes of Dewey."[16]

Converging pressures on education to prepare youth for work and maintain the nation's international economic hegemony, especially in the wake of Russia's Sputnik launch in 1957, led to intensified science, technology, engineering, and mathematics (STEM) instruction, bolstered by high-stakes assessment, at the expense of the humanities and social sciences. In the decades following, exaggerated claims about our declining competitive standing in the world tied to sluggish performance in high school STEM, coupled with anxiety about encroachment of values and beliefs in public schools, led to a steady reduction in class time devoted to the social studies and, concurrently, to growing disaffection with the bureaucracy of public schooling. Intersections of form and substance are striking: preoccupation with our global economic position coincided with efforts to import market-like models to public education and devolve curricular decisions to local control.*

---

* The fact that few, if any, of our international competitors—who allegedly outperformed us on standardized assessments—had much interest in market

Although it is hard to know which came first, the chicken of economic anxiety or the egg of school choice, the combination still gathers steam in communities uneasy about government generally and anxious about its role in decisions over what and how to teach innocent children. Multiplier effects of fear-mongering about loss of global hegemony and allergy to what demagogues call social engineering (if not socialism) are now painfully clear: growing inequality, racial resegregation of schools and neighborhoods, "me first" hoarding of opportunity, and erosion of faith in the American egalitarian experiment. Increased emphasis on STEM conveyed the message that hard skills ostensibly linked to future job opportunities were to be privileged over development of cognitive, behavioral, and moral foundations of civic life. It was a simple matter of there being only so many hours in the school day, and if we were going to focus more on STEM inevitably that would leave less time for history, social studies, geography, government, and whatever other components of civics were covered. Adding to this time-constraint problem were recurrent and heated ideological disputes over whether and how topics typically and erroneously assumed to be not as straightforward as science and math (e.g., history and literature) were to be included and taught. Data from the National Council for the Social Studies, its vested interests notwithstanding, provide evidence of erosion in the status and centrality of civics in K–12, a trend that has been blamed by some observers for the general decline in

---

solutions to public education was an irony missed by Americans advocating for choice, vouchers, and the like.

social cohesion and the ascendance of extremist forces that threaten democracy.[17]

Leaving aside the legitimacy and efficacy of holding schools accountable for all our current problems of democracy, the multipartisan outpouring of interest in reviving civics education is reassuring. But even now it is hard to discern if the advocates for reform have in mind a shift toward more formal "curricularization" and, if so, whether they account sufficiently for the constraining politics of education. If it is true that we are experiencing a swing back in the direction of political and moral goals of public education and away from its primary role as producer of "human capital," the next question is whether and how lessons from political economy can find a place in teacher preparation and in the high school curriculum. I turn to this question in chapter 3.

CURRICULUM OPTIONS
SCHOOLS OF THOUGHT

> Debate over purpose in public education has
> been a continuous process of creating and
> reshaping a democratic institution that . . .
> helped to create a democratic society.
>
> DAVID TYACK AND LARRY CUBAN

> Nobody goes there anymore—it's too
> crowded.
>
> YOGI BERRA

IN THE PRECEDING CHAPTERS, I offered a rationale for enriching civic education, in and out of school, with principles of
political economy or what is also known as public economics. Note here that "*civic* education," without the "s" suggests
that school-centered reform requires a concurrent strategy to

connect schools with their external constituents. Although this chapter focuses heavily on the revival of civics instruction *in schools*, it is worth underscoring again the importance of linking them to their external environments, which I will address in chapter 4.

To set the stage for realistic and enriched school-based civics curricula, a reminder about context. American education history provides ample evidence of the hazards faced by reformers who neglect to attend to the delicate balance between schools and their environments. To press this point further, it is not a random coincidence that pressures to revive civic education coincide with increasingly strained relations at the borders of schools and their communities. The converging pandemics of COVID-19, racial violence, and distrust of science have awakened us to the fragility of democracy; and they have fueled the latest rounds of bitter political fighting over the content and form of public instruction. Anyone who has attended a local school board meeting lately, and observed the rhetorically and at times physically violent interactions between parents and administrators—over such matters as the teaching of climate science and racial history or about the legitimacy of vaccine and mask requirements—can appreciate historian Lawrence Cremin's admonition: "Transformation of curricula . . . [involves] a continuing political process in which various lay publics, the several professions with a stake in schooling, and a variety of special-interest groups [participate] in a continuing redefinition of what a high school education [means]."[1]

FROM THE INSIDE OUT

I start with suggestions for how to infuse principles of political economy in school-based teaching—civics with the "s." There is no shortage of opinions about how to improve high school education, so any attempt to encourage or require new material, in this case focused on applications of theories of collective action and public goods, should start with a close look at the intended receptor sites: How is civics taught in high schools today and how are future teachers prepared to teach it? A key question is whether there is room in the already crowded high school agenda to add new material, and whether the suggestion can come without more badgering of teachers by outside experts. The question relates directly to the possibilities for enriched teacher preparation, especially given the pressures to shorten those programs in hopes of attracting more qualified candidates to the profession and making their careers economically more viable. To restate a source of my optimism for the proposed strategy, many candidates for licensure are already working in schools to satisfy practicum requirements, which means the lag between what they learn and when they get to use it is shorter than may be assumed.

Whether the content I recommend is best covered in government, the social studies, history, or STEM courses, or whether they should form the basis of a self-contained and "curricularized" program of civics instruction, continues to be debated among education researchers. That question is better left to teachers, their professional associations, the faculty involved in their professional preparation, and their trusted mentors. In terms of where to place the ideas in postsecondary educator-preparation programs, again I hesitate to be too prescriptive, though I would like to see them in courses for all future high school teachers, regardless of the subject they specialize in. (My orientation is toward programs in colleges and universities, where most teachers gain their professional credentials; hopefully the ideas will be welcomed also in nontraditional and residency programs that have become increasingly popular.)

What is the lay of the land today? Most states require some amount of civics at the high school level, although it is still more common to see the intended content listed under "general social studies" or "government" rather than in programs explicitly called "civics." Even though the content is not usually mandated separately, state standards typically include graduation requirements for some minimal number of credits in state and local government, with the expectation that such knowledge will promote greater civic understanding, responsibility, and participation. In Pennsylvania, for example, the wording is relatively detailed: "In all public, private or parochial schools, there shall be integrated in the social studies curriculum . . . three planned courses, each 120-clock hours . . . [covering] history and government of the United States as provided in section 1605 of the Public School Code of 1949."

The Pennsylvania mandate goes on to specify that

> during grades seven through twelve inclusive, there shall be included at least four semesters or equivalent study in the history and government of that portion of America which has become the United

States of America, and of the Commonwealth of Pennsylvania, of such nature, kind or quality, as to have for its purpose the developing, teaching and presentation of the principles and ideals of the American republican representative form of government, as portrayed and experienced by the acts and policies of the framers of the Declaration of Independence and framers of the Constitution of the United States and the Bill of Rights. The study of the history of the United States, including the study of the Constitution of the United States and the study of the history and Constitution of this Commonwealth, shall also be such as will emphasize the good, worthwhile and best features and points of the social, economic and cultural development, the growth of the American family life, high standard of living of the United States citizen, the privileges enjoyed by such citizens, their heritage and its derivations of and in our principles of government. Such instruction shall have for its purpose also the instilling into every boy and girl who comes out of our public, private and parochial schools their solemn duty and obligation to exercise intelligently their voting privilege and to understand the advantages of the American republican form of government as compared with various other forms of government.*

---

* The word "mandate," when applied to masks and vaccines, arouses anger and suspicion among politicians and others who fear coercive government intrusion in personal liberties; many of those same politicians, however, have no problem drafting and enacting mandates—with harsh penalties for

State rules elsewhere cover similar ground, with greater or lesser specificity. In Wisconsin, for example, curriculum content is somewhat vaguely worded: "Graduation requirements include three credits of social studies including state and local government." But the *testing* requirement is strict: "Starting with the class of 2017, in order to receive a diploma from a Wisconsin public school, students must pass 60 of 100 questions identical to the US Citizen and Immigration Services citizenship exam." (Among the issues differentiating state strategies for education, the role of testing always looms large, and whether the exams are or should be used as proxies for curriculum content is a matter of almost constant debate.)

Varying policies and mandates across the country are subject to change, which further complicates efforts to track the information consistently. According to data compiled by the Tufts University Center for Information and Research on Civic Learning and Engagement (CIRCLE), as of 2012 Iowa had no required social studies courses and no state assessment in social studies, but the Education Commission of the States (ECS) reports that "beginning with the 2010–2011 school year graduating class, all students in schools and school districts [in Iowa] shall satisfactorily complete at least three units

---

noncompliance—governing how certain subjects are taught in public schools. Since 2022, more than 30 states have introduced or adopted laws restricting teaching of race and racism. See Stout and Wilburn 2022. According to *Science* magazine, "At least 25 states have considered legislation that would limit or eliminate DEI programs or otherwise constrain ways in which universities could teach about related topics." See Thorp 2023a. These developments reflect the autocratic, rather than libertarian, impulses in modern conservatism, a transition discussed briefly in the introduction to this book.

of social studies." ECS claims that as of 2016 all fifty states and the District of Columbia had mandates requiring teaching of social studies.[2]

Along with state rules and requirements for course-taking generally, nongovernmental organizations have played an important role. The well-known Advanced Placement (AP) program of the College Board, a prominent nonprofit organization with hundreds of college and university members, continues to provide curricula in a wide range of topics. Most colleges and universities award credit and use AP test results for placement of students: "As of fall 2021, 32 states [had] implemented statewide or systemwide AP credit policies, which typically require all public higher education institutions to award credit for AP Exam scores of 3 or higher. . . . Over the past 10 years, the percentage of U.S. public high school graduates who took an AP Exam during high school has increased, as has the percentage of U.S. public high school graduates who scored a 3 or higher on at least one AP Exam." One of the most popular courses in the AP portfolio, "American Government and Politics," covers a broad set of topics relevant to civics and citizenship. The curriculum (tied to the exam) is organized in units covering foundations of American democracy, interactions among branches of government, civil liberties and civil rights, political ideologies and beliefs, and political participation. A good place to add emphasis on collective action and public goods would be in classes labeled "ideology and economic policy" and "balancing minority and majority rights." The Advanced Placement system includes topics that are perhaps not as easily identifiable as related to civics, such as studio art and design, but that involve a complex interplay of values, tastes, and preferences and that hint at experiential opportunities for students to engage with the subtleties of civic engagement and responsibility.[3]

High school teaching requirements have a direct impact on the scope and substance of education preparation programs, for obvious reasons: criteria for licensure reflect state mandates, if not directly then at least thematically. Like so much else in the education landscape of the United States, teacher preparation is a diffused and diverse business. According to the American Association of Colleges of Teacher Education (AACTE), as of 2016 one-third of all US postsecondary institutions awarded roughly 300,000 degrees and certificates for future teachers, with about half at the master's (postgraduate) level, a third going to undergraduates, and the remainder in certificates and doctoral degrees. Candidates for licensure in elementary and early childhood education tend to be concentrated at the undergraduate level, while future teachers in social studies and the sciences are often required by their state licensing authorities to acquire preservice training in MA and doctoral programs. This divide reflects a balancing of pedagogical and content knowledge, to borrow from Lee Shulman's classic formulation of the (blended) components of teaching proficiency. But there is considerable overlap, as some elementary and special-education programs are housed in graduate schools of education. Some of the best educator preparation, especially in areas requiring advanced content knowledge such as history or economics or politics, happens in graduate training programs. On the other hand, it is also true that in liberal arts colleges that include opportunities for undergraduates to prepare for teaching careers, there is often a reliance on faculty in the various disciplines to provide content-specific input. (I will return in chapter 4 to my suggestion that by focusing on teacher education programs in universities we might cultivate new and fruitful collaborations between pedagogical experts and their colleagues in the other academic disciplines.)[4]

Macro-level overviews of where civics is taught and how future teachers are prepared suggest there is fertile, albeit rocky, ground for planting of new curricular concepts drawn from political economy. To address the question of where and how to integrate them in secondary teacher preparation programs, it is again important to acknowledge the diversity reflected in the highly individualized syllabi written and used by teacher educators in colleges and universities. A glimpse at such syllabi can be helpful. Take, for example, a course for graduate students working toward secondary school licensure in the social studies. An excerpt from the description of one well-designed course lays out themes and expectations:

> This course is designed to support social studies teachers in developing a knowledge base about social studies curriculum and pedagogy. The course focuses on preparing teachers for the process of navigating state standards, school priorities, and student needs and interests when deciding what and how to teach. Students will examine the development of the social studies curriculum and the current standards and debates within the field. They will also develop a better understanding of and the skills

necessary to engage students in inquiry into social issues. Special attention will be paid to designing inquiry-based units and to instructional methods that support student inquiry.

It is worth noting that this approach to preparing future social studies teachers embodies blends of content and pedagogical knowledge to be learned through formal and experiential instruction. For example, students in this course are expected to study required texts (such as those of Lesh, Rubin, Swan et al., and Hess and McAvoy) and also to carry out practice-oriented assignments such as, "Map out a unit plan that aims to engage students in inquiry into a significant social issue or concept through the study of a [District of Columbia Public Schools] or [Virginia] social studies standard of your choosing." Teacher candidates are asked to make use of local resources such as museums and historical sites where "as a teacher [you and] your students together [will] try to make sense of the political, social, historical, and economic contexts of our world." The course plan includes modules on addressing difficult issues, engaging students in discussions of controversial topics, and historical thinking. With some adjustment, it seems plausible to integrate into such a syllabus lessons drawn from models of collective action and public goods and, as I will show later in this chapter, to do so in a way that motivates a blend of theoretical and experiential understanding of those concepts. Ideally, candidates seeking secondary school licensure would leave with a richer array of concepts ripe for translation into specific instructional techniques relevant to the schools and students with whom they will work.

In another syllabus designed by a respected social studies teacher educator, a goal is to "acquaint the student with issues, trends, philosophies, methods, materials, organization, and basic instructional procedures in social studies education." And the scope is broad:

> [Students will] understand and apply different methods for teaching [the] social studies in middle and high school; demonstrate expertise in the psychology and sociology of teaching students in the midst of adolescent development in a multicultural environment; provide a sound foundation for teaching social studies courses including World Geography, Economics, Philosophy, World History, American Government, Psychology, and Sociology; and enhance an understanding by the student of issues, trends, philosophies, methods, materials, organization, and basic instructional procedures in social studies education; and enhance an awareness of multicultural education and other relevant social trends and issues.

Assignments included in this ambitious one-semester course provide opportunities for candidates to develop ways for their future students to "draw warranted conclusions about the causes of (reasons for) social [phenomena] (historical, geographic, economic, etc.)." Of perhaps greatest relevance to the possibility of infusing principles of political economy, the syllabus includes an assignment to develop a mini-lesson on a "structured academic controversy," with specific reference to economic concepts.

A similar approach is found in the syllabus for a course entitled "Teaching Historical, Civic, Geographic, and Economic Thinking for Social Studies," currently offered at the University of Wisconsin. The emphasis here is on preparing students to develop lessons and assessments "to teach social studies for democratic and global citizenship in diverse classrooms . . . [and] make connections between educational theory and the use of different pedagogical strategies." I refer to this example because it seems to provide another potentially hospitable place to integrate principles of political economy: a goal of the course is to have future teachers consider "the role of geographic, *economic*, historical, and *political* contexts on current events and issues (e.g., global conflicts, policy decisions, management of environmental issues, migration) [and] how these issues are framed differently depending on geography and power dynamics" (italics added). Again, in the effort to infuse more content in an already dense learning agenda, syllabi such as this one, with explicit mention of economics and politics, seem ready for attention to issues such as climate change and environmental protection, education policy, and other areas where individual choice may yield socially suboptimal outcomes.[5]

For an example of how civics is included in STEM, consider a syllabus designed to prepare future teachers of high school earth science. As I have argued elsewhere, the tensions between STEM and other valued topics vying for coverage in the secondary school curriculum make possibilities for synergy especially attractive. This course is structured around the core themes of the National Science Education Standards as well as the requirements that were in place in Michigan at least going back to 2006. As shown in box 4, this course covers content and pedagogy and, more importantly, integrates *principles of scientific inquiry and its social context.* This formulation of the goals and process for preparing high school STEM teachers opens rich opportunities for integration of lessons from the political economy of collective action generally, and challenges of science policy—including ethics and the uses of research—specifically.

Box 4 adapts core principles and themes in the latest version of the Next Generation Science Standards (NGSS), an ongoing project of the National Academies of Sciences, Engineering, and Medicine, the National Science Teachers Association, the American Association for the Advancement of Science, and Achieve (an organization created with private philanthropic funding to advance the basic notions of standards-based reform). The NGSS builds on a model of "three-dimensional learning," covering scientific and engineering practices, crosscutting concepts, and disciplinary core ideas; attempts to link scientific principles to real-world situations; and applies findings from advanced cognitive research on "learning progressions."

 BOX 4. STANDARDS FOR SCIENCE TEACHER PREPARATION
STANDARD 1: CONTENT

- Know and understand the major concepts and principles of the teaching discipline(s) as defined by state and national standards of the science education community.
- Know and understand major concepts and principles unifying science disciplines.

- Design, conduct and report investigations within a science discipline.
- Apply mathematics in problem-solving and scientific investigation.

STANDARD 2: NATURE OF SCIENCE

- Know and understand the philosophical nature of science and the conventions of scientific explanation.
- Engage K–12 students effectively in studies of the nature of science and conventions of scientific explanation.

STANDARD 3: INQUIRY

- Know and understand scientific inquiry and its relationship to the development of scientific knowledge.
- Engage K–12 students effectively in scientific inquiry appropriate for their grade level and abilities.

STANDARD 4: CONTEXT OF SCIENCE

- Know and understand the relationship of science to other human values and endeavors.
- Engage K–12 students effectively in the study of the relationship of science to other human values and endeavors.
- Relate science to the personal lives needs and interests of K–12 students.

STANDARD 5: SKILLS OF TEACHING

- Use diverse and effective actions, strategies and methodologies to teach science.

- Interact effectively with K–12 students to promote learning and demonstrate student achievement.
- Organize and manage science activities effectively in different student groupings.
- Use advanced technology to teach K–12 students science.
- Use prior conceptions and K–12 student interests to promote learning.

STANDARD 6: CURRICULUM

- Develop coherent, meaningful goals, plans, and materials and find resources.
- Relate plans and resources to professionally-developed state and national standards, including the National Science Education Standards.
- Plan and develop science curriculum addressing the needs, interests and abilities of all pre-K–12 students.

STANDARD 7: SOCIAL CONTEXT

- Know and understand the values and needs of the community and their effect on the teaching and learning of science.
- Use community human and institutional resources to advance the learning of science in the classroom and field.

STANDARD 8: ASSESSMENT

- Align science goals, instruction and outcomes.

- Know and use a variety of contemporary science assessment strategies to determine pre-K–12 student needs and levels of learning and development.
- Use assessment appropriately to determine, guide and change science instruction.

STANDARD 9: ENVIRONMENT FOR LEARNING

- Create and maintain a psychologically and socially safe and supportive learning environment.
- Manage the activities and materials of science safely in storage areas, labs and field.
- Keep and use living organisms as in the classroom in a safe, ethical and appropriate manner.

STANDARD 10: PROFESSIONAL PRACTICE

- Know and participate in professional organizations and activities of the science education community beyond the classroom.
- Behave ethically and in best interests of pre-K–12 students and the community.
- Engage in reflective practices and make continuous efforts to improve in practice.
- Work willingly with peers, supervisors and others in a professional manner

★ *Source*: Eastern Michigan University 2006.

A final example with a strong STEM-civics connection focuses on *data science*, a relatively new term that covers mathematics of measurement and estimation, technical aspects of collecting and analyzing quantitative information, and, in its more enlightened definition, ethical and policy implications of using different types of data for different purposes. It is perhaps painfully obvious that in the age of COVID-19, personal and social risk assessment that influences individual and governmental decisions requires subtle appreciation for the virtues—and limits—of epidemiological and other large-scale data. Disparities in the health effects of COVID-19 across racial and economic groups make it even more important to attend to these issues. Indeed, how such information is reported to the general public is in itself a controversial question that warrants focus in civics instruction. Here I am thinking of the tension between social media as a putatively democratizing technology, on the one hand, and the antisocial effects of instant dissemination of unfounded claims and conspiracy-mongering that pollutes the internet, on the other. (Uncurated information can have negative externalities.)

As argued in a thoughtful syllabus used as part of secondary school educator preparation at Stanford, "The ability to work with, understand, and use data has already become an essential life skill and a requirement for an ever-expanding range of jobs and careers. It is becoming imperative that both the current and next generation of educators be aware of these changes and prepared for teaching students to thoughtfully engage with data." Professor Victor Lee's course as it was offered in 2022, "Teaching Data Science in Secondary School," introduces to future secondary schoolteachers relevant content knowledge on tools, platforms, and data environments, as well as at least a basic understanding of artificial intelligence and machine learning. The course also spends time on complex questions at the intersection of data science and society, such as the effects of "big data" on inequality and democracy. As we have seen in other syllabi for secondary schoolteaching, the data science example includes readings from theoretical literature but also innovative experiential assignments: "You should design a task for the student to think through . . . making inferences from a data representation, explaining their ideas of how a data process works to produce a given visualization, how businesses collect and use personal data, or the *ethics of data*" (italics added). It should be possible in such a course to include at least some discussion of theories of individual rights, social goods, and the political economy of collective action.[6]

PEDAGOGY BY EXAMPLE: "THE THREE Rs" REDUX

Real-estate brokers like to remind buyers that the three principles of residential markets are "location, location, location." In pedagogy, a similar rule might apply: the three most important rules for engaging youth in understanding and applying theoretical knowledge are "relevance, relevance, relevance." Here I will make an argument for adapting lessons from political economy for teacher preparation and high school civics, focusing on four familiar challenges that should resonate with students of all ages. Other cases can and should be developed. In each of the cases outlined below, my hope would be for teacher educators to collaborate closely with colleagues in other departments, such as economics, sociology, history, politics, psychology, business, computer science, mathematics, and law. In addition to providing future teachers the enriched perspective that comes from interdisciplinary scholarship of the sort proposed, the effect could very well be to reinforce mutually respectful ties across campus, with broad benefits to the university's mission and reputation.

Case 1: School Choice . . . and Consequences

Arguments for and against charter schools and voucher systems often turn into polemics of ideology, adorned selectively with findings from research of varying quality and limited generalizability. One obstacle preventing resolution of the main question—whether and under what conditions the governance of public schooling might be modified in the direction of markets and away from traditional bureaucratic control—is confusion over the dependent variable: what values and outcomes of education matter most? Advocates for choice often rely on data showing that poor and marginalized communities are not well served by their existing neighborhood schools and, unlike their more affluent neighbors who can afford to send their kids to private or religious schools, they are stuck in a system that perpetuates and exacerbates resource disparities and achievement gaps. Differences in average scores on standardized tests of reading and math, for example, between students in traditional and charter schools, especially when other explanatory factors are "controlled" experimentally, are entered as evidence of the relative advantages of one system over the other, although limitations in method and metrics preclude definitive answers. The fervency with which claims and counterclaims are expressed, however, usually exceeds the "carrying capacity" of the data.*

A different argument centers on other purposes of schooling, in particular its role in shaping and sustaining pluralist norms and fulfilling promises of egalitarianism enshrined in our founding documents. Recall from chapter 2 the distinction between the human capital (product) and moral/political (process) goals of public education. Opponents of choice worry about the downside risks of dismantling a system that aspires, at least theoretically, to building an ethos of community, equity, and opportunity in our multicultural society. Quantitative data (not limited to test scores) are marshaled to suggest that the potential social cost of choice systems which, for example, reinforce "hoarding" impulses of the wealthy and lead to resegregation along economic and racial lines, is too high a price to pay even if test scores of disadvantaged youth are shown to rise. Conflicts arising from different approaches to balancing subgroup progress against broader and unintended social consequences are not amenable to empirical resolution: where values are at stake, the stakes are high (and the arguments heated).[7]

If the debate over school choice and vouchers sounds familiar, as a case of individual choice colliding with collective outcomes, that is the point. And it is not new: although the controversy has been especially sharp in the last thirty years,

---

* I commend Henry Braun for this lovely turn of phrase in his Lindquist Lecture, American Educational Research Association, San Diego, 2021. Among efforts to untangle the effects of choice on achievement outcomes, the work of Macke Raymond and colleagues is notable.

thanks to ascendance of market thinking in education policy and its opponents who are nervous about the so-called neo-liberal agenda, one of the most painful battles occurred more than fifty years ago in New York City. A remarkable experiment in "decentralization," funded by the Ford Foundation, aimed to give poor and largely Black citizens of Ocean Hill-Brownsville and other sections of the nation's biggest and most sprawling metropolis an alternative to the unconscionably bad educational opportunities they had endured for decades. The ensuing drama brought about the longest teacher strike in New York history. (Cinema buffs may remember the opening scene in Woody Allen's *Sleeper:* when a cryogenically frozen man is thawed out, he looks around at the devasted landscape and asks, "What happened?" The answer: "A man by the name of Albert Shanker [head of the teachers' union in New York] got the atom bomb.") The strike and all its attendant political rhetoric in the street and on the airwaves led to a rupture between traditional allies. Predominantly white and Jewish teachers who had fought for civil rights, marched against the Vietnam War, and believed in labor rights and due process suddenly found themselves battling traditional partners demanding educational equity.*

The fight over decentralization—intended to free parents and children from the stultifying bureaucracy of the

---

* As a high school student in Queens, I experienced the trauma of 1968 firsthand. It was a transformative event for me, many of my peers, and for some of our most beloved teachers who were torn between their allegiance to principles of labor rights and their commitment to correcting centuries of racial injustice. The damage to Black-Jewish relations, in New York and beyond, was a tragic consequence of the whole affair.

largest school district in the nation—was a precursor to decades of battle over the moral legitimacy and political sustainability of our public school system. Public school students and their families, especially those in urban areas hardest hit with economic and racial disparity, encounter and cope with the underlying tension to this day, and because political aspirants and leaders at all levels of government inevitably make it an electoral issue, its relevance makes for an excellent case.[8]

In capable hands of educators interested in presenting the essence of the conflict, the history of choice as a mechanism for desegregation can motivate appreciation for complexities of private behavior and social consequences that go beyond the specifics of school reform. Here is one way to tell the story and motivate consideration of its implications— which would benefit from co-teaching by faculty in mathematics and/or simulation methods.

Developed by the polymath (and later Nobel laureate) Thomas Schelling in the mid-1970s, his checkerboard model is another example in the genre of the "remorseless logic" of well-intentioned rationality. Squares on a checkerboard represent residences; two groups with distinguishable features (for example, race, ethnicity, or economic status) occupy those residences, and the eight squares that surround each square represent an individual's neighborhood. Individuals assess their neighborhood situation and are assumed to be able to move to a different location more compatible with their preferences for neighborhood heterogeneity. For example, if both groups prefer to have at least half of their neighbors alike, but an individual is currently in a square that does not satisfy this criterion, then that individual will move to a different square on the board that achieves or exceeds the 50 percent level. Every time an individual moves, he or she changes the composition of adjoining neighborhoods, forcing the occupants of those neighborhoods to reassess their situations and move or stay accordingly. Each individual's satisfaction, therefore, is conditional upon the actions of others.

A dramatic prediction of this individual choice model is that even if we assume that individuals prefer more heterogeneity, the final aggregated outcome is persistent separation. Applying this logic to decisions of parents vis-à-vis their children's schools, it is easy to see how progressive instincts for heterogeneity may not be sufficient to guarantee the desired outcome. (Obviously this is more interesting than the case in which people choose segregation—models of "white flight" have different baseline assumptions.) As shown in figure 4, simulations of the checkerboard game yield disturbing results: even if parents want their kids to attend integrated schools, the outcome fails in a system of free mobility.

Having used this model in a graduate course on education policy, I see its potential value in educator preparation and, ultimately, in high school classrooms. Like the prisoner's dilemma, it can be an eye-opener, a challenge to young people (and their teachers!) who are perhaps puzzled by the realities of their own educational (and residential) settings. When I taught the Schelling story in the late 1990s, we used a physical checkerboard; now there are digital versions available online, which may be more natural for today's generation. In any case, it is incumbent on educators to ask the relevant

	X	X		0	X	X	
X	X	X	0	0	0	X	X
X	X	0	0			0	X
X	0		0		0	0	0
0	0	0	X	0	0	0	
	0	X	X	X	0	0	0
	X	X	X	X			
0	0					X	

FIGURE 4. Schelling checkerboard, heterogeneity unsatisfied. This figure shows the unfortunate outcome of a set of egalitarian choices: each individual wants something more than a third of its neighbors to be like itself. In the end, most individuals occupy a square that has a satisfactory neighborhood, but when the board is viewed as a whole, the community is segregated.
Source: My description here of the Schelling model is drawn (largely verbatim) from a paper coauthored with three students in my Georgetown University policy class. See Feuer et al. 1997. The title of that paper borrows from Schelling 1978. I am grateful to Victor Lee for pointing me to a digitized application: see https://ncase.me/polygons/.

follow-up questions: How remorseless is the logic of the checkerboard? What happens if the assumption of individual choice is modified to allow for the possibility that small groups of families will work together toward a shared goal? How might government interventions, whether through incentives or more coercive school-attendance rules, limit the downside risks while enabling the moral and educational benefits of choice? What types of collective action might prevent the worst social outcomes? Ever the optimist about the virtues of public policy, my hope is that creative suggestions for what to do might sprout from this otherwise dismal model.

Case 2: Free Choice and Free Riders

In chapter 2, I mentioned climate change and environmental degradation as examples of externalities. Because (thankfully) many high school youth are worried about the sustainability of our planet as we have known it, and because so many of them are justifiably frustrated by the slow pace of progress toward reducing toxic emissions, the pedagogical challenge is whether framing the problem in terms of the commons and its tragedies might provide fresh insights and, more importantly, tools for future decision makers.

The basic story is straightforward. Clean water and air are essentially "public goods," in both the moral and economic meanings of the term. Although not mentioned specifically in the US Constitution (or other such documents in the world), the right to breathe and the right to consume safe water are viewed by most people as so basic to biological and ecological existence that they do not need additional discussion or justification. In a word, there is a moral basis to ensuring a safe environment. But as we know from the logic of the commons, morality can sometimes collide with rationality, which is where political economy comes in. Simply put, are we willing to take a chance that people with good intentions about the quality of the environment will be motivated sufficiently to behave in ways that contribute meaningfully to the public good—especially if that means paying an individual price that may seem too high?*

To motivate this discussion in high school classes, it may be best to start with a simple experiment. Involving faculty from the chemistry department and business school would make it even more interesting. Have one student in the class play the role of an automobile salesperson, and other students play the role of new car buyers. The salesperson shows the buyers two options: an electric car with advanced technology that reduces hydrocarbon emissions and a more familiar car that runs on gasoline but is considerably less expensive. Students who have had some chemistry will appreciate the scientific aspects of this situation. And all students will quickly come to realize that fundamentally it is not a technical problem as much as a social or economic problem: Why would a rational buyer choose the more expensive car? Here I would encourage a kind of "talk-aloud" segment in the class and have students verbalize their thought process in deciding which car to buy. A predictable conversation might go something like this: "I really want to make a difference to the quality of the air we breathe, and would be willing to pay extra to know I am making such a difference. But I'm only buying one car, and from my understanding of the chemistry I know that will have almost no effect on the overall situation. So, I'm just not sure this is a good use of my money."

---

* Good drinking water, unlike fresh air, is more easily provided through the private market. It is worth noting, though, that the externality associated with nonrecyclable plastic water bottles.

The salesperson is prepared for this response, and tells the student buyer, "Yes, I appreciate your logic, and I'm glad to say that in fact *you are not alone*—just today I've sold 100 cars with pollution mitigation technology, so in fact you could contribute to a real improvement!" So now the student-buyer, being a rational thinker, has a new challenge: "If everyone else is buying the more expensive car, then the air quality is likely to improve whether I'm part of that group or not." In other words, the student who in every other part of his or her educational experience is encouraged to think analytically and rationally, now has to manage the cognitive dissonance that worried Garrett Hardin and others: the rational strategy conflicts with the morally preferred course of action. Put somewhat more cynically, the smart student sees a chance to become a "free-rider," a beneficiary of clean air made possible by the deeds of peers who are apparently willing to pay the extra costs.*

At this point the role of the teacher becomes crucial, and with a bit of theatrical preparation can assume the role of government policy maker or legislator authorized to enact some kind of intervention to avoid what is by now an obviously bad outcome—namely, failure of the market for environmentally friendlier cars. Borrowing from the real world of environmental protection as a legitimate place for coercive governmental action, the teacher can present the case for a mandate, a legally enforceable rule that prohibits sales of cars without the antipollution technology, and provide data to

---

* Other factors obviously enter into the decision: owning a high-end electric car has become a kind of status thing, suggesting that over time even somewhat self-interest-seeking impulses can result in social improvements.

show how, even though each consumer's choice has been abridged, in the aggregate everyone is better off. A well-prepared teaching team will be ready to present the relevant history—from the early days of the Environmental Protection Agency, policy was motivated by the simple analytics of externalities and free-rider effects—and the relevant data indicating that the quality of the air has actually improved.

Showing the remorseless logic of market failure, though, while necessary, is not sufficient. What must come next is creative discussion of potential remedies: are government mandates the only or best way to curb the downside risks of individual self-interest? Especially in a society such as ours, with so much consternation about government overreach and encroachment on cherished individual rights, are there other ways to move in the direction of socially desirable outcomes with less infringement on personal choice and the workings of the business economy?

Here the work of the Nobel laureate William Nordhaus would be my choice for what to emphasize. Nordhaus has been a staunch advocate for reframing the climate debate away from reliance either on strict government mandates or extremist faith in free markets. As he eloquently argued in a *New York Times* interview, "We see all around us the miracles of the marketplace. But this does not apply to public goods . . . in a well-managed society we must recognize the need for collective actions as well as actions of the private sector. To deal with collective action when it comes to public goods will require some kind of government intervention." What kinds of government intervention does he recommend? One that affects the supply side—federal support for development of advanced carbon-reducing technologies—and one that affects the demand side—increasing the price of polluting. "In my own mind," continues Nordhaus, "there is a twin set of policies. One is carbon pricing and one is strong support for low-carbon technologies. Both are necessary if we're going to reach our goals. Carbon pricing by itself is not sufficient. By itself, it won't bring forth the necessary technologies. Carbon pricing needs the helping hand of government support of new low-carbon technologies."[9]

Creative teachers can motivate students to appreciate these principles with the common sense of dollars and cents. How high should the carbon tax (or what Nordhaus calls the carbon price) be set? Are there potentially regressive aspects of such a policy, given that a disproportional share of the tax burden is likely to fall on lower-income people? How much will it cost taxpayers to invest public funds in new technology? What is of great interest here, again, is the synergy between what is viewed as essentially a moral or civic problem—saving the environment—and the scientific basis both for understanding the inevitable effects of the internal combustion engine and the mathematics of public goods. Making such a module required for STEM and non-STEM majors, therefore, would add value to civics as it is currently taught. Time permitting, the teaching team can follow the logic into other areas, such as the debate over mandates in the Affordable Care Act, the tension between religious freedom and public health that required Supreme Court adjudication, and other such examples.[10]

Case 3: The Remorseless Logic of Road Congestion

Student drivers, like the rest of us, prefer to get where they are going on time. Inevitably, though, they will encounter soon after passing their road test a situation that will give pause (literally). It is such a ubiquitous phenomenon that by now most people know it by one of its colloquial names, "rubbernecking" or, in Philadelphia, "gaper block." Traffic in (say) the northbound lanes of the highway comes to a creeping halt, until cars pass the point where, *in the southbound lanes,* a terrible accident has occurred, and police and ambulances are attempting to provide relief. In other words, no physical obstruction caused northbound drivers to be delayed, but rather something on the other side of the median divider led to what seems like nightmarishly inescapable congestion. Aside from anxieties about arriving late to class or a meeting, and annoyance at the lack of any obvious way to end the traffic jam, can the experience motivate a broader understanding of the tension between individual rationality and social irrationality?

Thanks again to Thomas Schelling, there is a neat way to teach this story. As he explained in an essay in his *Micromotives and Macrobehavior* (1978), looking at the situation from the perspective of individual drivers can be illuminating. Upon seeing an accident happening in the oncoming lanes, the first driver slows down just long enough to satisfy normal curiosity; the rational calculus here is that a few seconds of delay is a cost the driver is willing to bear. The driver directly behind, though, has a more limited choice: he or she must slow down to avoid ramming into the rear of the car ahead, which turns those few seconds the first driver was willing to pay into a longer delay for the second driver. Students will quickly appreciate where this is going: the cumulative burden to what was a rationally understandable decision by one curious and safety-conscious driver grows perhaps exponentially so that twenty and thirty and one hundred cars back everyone is losing much more precious time than they might have bargained for. Few of them would concede that the benefit of seeing what's going on across the divide justifies that high a cost. For added spice to this story, consider the thought process of drivers who have had the delay forced upon them: "Since I've already paid the price, I may as well have a look." Again, the logic seems remorseless: suboptimal outcomes derive from good (or at least not intentionally harmful) acts carried out by well-informed and rational actors.

When I taught this story in a required MBA class (at Drexel University) on science and society, one of my co-instructors, an engineer, insisted there was a technological solution to the problem, though he had trouble coming up with the formula. I somewhat generously (and with obvious technical naïveté) went along with the suggestion and speculated that if all cars were equipped with a device allowing drivers to communicate with one another, they might be able to reach a fair market solution to the traffic jam: How much would any driver be willing to pay others to speed up and not rubberneck? In the back of my mind, I worried about the transaction costs of this strategy and barriers to enforcing what would end up being a nearly infinite number of bilateral contracts—remembering again the institutional economics rebuttal of the Coase theorem—but in any case my idea did not receive much praise either from students in the class or from my engineer colleague. Instead, the conclusion we reached, sadly, was that looking for a technical solution was a fool's errand and that it made more sense to understand the problem through the lens of collective action, the limits of free choice, and, especially important, the inadequacy of any obvious governmental or other imposed solution.

The last point should become a key part of the lesson because we know from decades of complaining about rubbernecking that most interventions are woefully unsatisfying. Sending state troopers to the scene—on the side where the rubbernecking happens—is a typical response that has almost no effect. These fine public servants wave frantically to get drivers to *not* slow down (an unnatural act for police whose more customary contribution to public safety is actually to discourage speeding), but the effect on congestion is minimal at best. Another form of intervention is to inform all drivers that there has been an accident and to plead with them to keep going or choose another route. Before GPS systems provided such data, we had helicopters overhead with radio announcers sharing the news at least to drivers tuned in to the relevant frequencies. Traffic reporters' pleas to keep moving fall on mostly deaf ears, and come too late for most drivers to exit the highway and find another route. Yet another solution is to build high walls separating the two directions of traffic in hopes of preventing drivers from seeing the other side and reacting accordingly; whether the hoped-for benefits in terms of reduced delays is worth the cost of erecting such walls, not to mention the degradation of scenery and infringement of drivers' rights to see what they want, is not clear.

What are the takeaways from this lesson? First, that civic-minded drivers might remember the story and curb their curiosity when confronting a potential rubbernecking situation. Will people who have been made aware of the social effects of their action be motivated to act differently? Maybe. Second, neither markets nor bureaucracies alone can be expected to solve certain classes of commons problems, but a combination of public awareness and creative intervention might be helpful. In particular, I would encourage instructors in such a class to offer students a prize for coming up with creative remedies: maybe budding computer scientists will invent an app that sends proof to the motor vehicle authority of a driver's decision to forego the look-to-the-other-side and to get a financial reward for that choice. This might involve a variation of the E-ZPass technology now used in major highway systems, which substantially reduces tollgate congestion. The surveillance aspects of such a solution are not trivial. And of course, the third message from the traffic story is about the general problems of choice and consequences, which future decision makers will find handy when confronting many issues in everyday life.

Case 4: Affirmative Action: The Commons Inverted

High school students anticipating college are acutely aware of the imperfections of the applications and admissions process and understandably worry about the fairness of a system that rations scarce academic and institutional resources. Especially for those hoping to attend one of the more elite and selective private institutions, where the odds of entry are only marginally better than winning a state lottery, the debate over what criteria should be used by admissions officers involves a blend of moral, statistical, legal, and economic reasoning. It would take much more than a one-semester civics class to untangle all the complexities, but discussion of affirmative action and preferential admissions can be framed as a case of tensions between individual rights and social aspirations, and would resonate well with aspiring college-goers.

The meaning of affirmative action has evolved from its origins in 1960s and 1970s labor and civil rights laws. Today it is mainly understood as the effort to correct imbalances in racial, ethnic, and gender diversity, on college campuses as well as government and private organizations. Efforts by colleges and universities to include race, national origin, and gender as legitimate criteria in sorting and selecting among masses of applicants have been under fire for decades. Race-conscious admissions, in particular, has led to a series of lawsuits and US Supreme Court decisions, starting in 1974 (*DeFunis v. Odegaard*) and continuing to the present day. In the *Bakke* decision (1978), the court ruled that racial quotas violated civil rights law but that pursuit of a diverse student body provided a "compelling state interest" for the use of race-conscious admissions criteria. Challenges since then, therefore, have largely centered on the evidence concerning the diversity criterion and whether it justifies potential violations of individuals' civil rights. Two cases involving the University of Michigan, both decided in 2003, upheld key pieces of the *Bakke* decision, with further refinements to the principles of compelling interest and the requirement of "strict scrutiny" to be applied in adjudicating such controversies (the ruling essentially overturned its 1978 decision supporting the case brought in *Hopwood v. Texas*).[11]

The most recent cases, decided by the Supreme Court in June 2023, were brought by students claiming discrimination against Asian applicants (Harvard) and against Asian and white applicants (University of North Carolina), for the sake of increasing admissions of Black and Hispanic students. In anticipation of a ruling for plaintiffs, college administrators started to plan alternative procedures to sustain their commitment to diversity. They were right: although the 237-page decision hinted that universities could consider "diversity statements" of applicants that mention their race, Chief Justice Roberts warned that schools still can't use race in and of itself in determining admissions. In a rebuke of precedent that had been in place for nearly fifty years, the court ruled that diversity was no longer compelling enough to compromise the equal protection clause of the Fourteenth Amendment, which they decreed was violated by Harvard and UNC. Individual rights trumped [*sic*] the social good.[12]

Beyond the specifics of the cases decided in 2023, the underlying issues will be with us for a long time to come. Indeed, to say the question of preferential treatment in higher education is fraught with tension qualifies for the understatement of the year award. For high school students and their families, who have abundant opportunities to hear and participate in heated arguments for and against race-conscious admissions, the added value of including the topic in classroom pedagogy hinges on the willingness and ability of teachers to approach the question and its multiple layers not with an intent to proselytize for a particular point of view, but rather to equip young people with an analytical toolkit for them to use in reaching their own decisions. For this module it would be good to have teacher educators team up with law faculty knowledgeable in constitutional theory.

Let's start with the moral argument. In its original formulation, as articulated first by President Kennedy in 1961, affirmative action was about correcting historical injustice. President Johnson, with the added backing of the 1964 Civil Rights Act, solidified the argument in a speech to the graduating class of Howard University in 1965, which included these famous words: "You do not wipe away the scars of centuries by saying, 'Now you are free to go where you want, do as you desire, and choose the leaders you please.' You do not take a man who for years has been hobbled by chains, liberate him, bring him to the starting line of a race, saying, 'You are free to compete with all the others,' and still justly believe you have been completely fair." The history of Black people in America is, for many citizens regardless of their race or ethnicity, sufficient to justify large-scale interventions aimed at repairing past damage and pursuing principles of fairness codified in the elegant but unfulfilled promises of our founding documents. Johnson's words, however, went further, by emphasizing that the rhetoric of fairness is insufficient without steps to ensure that traditionally marginalized, underrepresented, and persecuted groups are given extra chances to succeed. That's the meaning of "affirmative"—assuring fairness by legislating a guarantee of completely equal treatment is not enough. Without necessarily going any further, this formulation of the problem will almost surely arouse classroom discussion. Were I the instructor, I would invoke the immortal words of Rabbi

Abraham Joshua Heschel, that "in a free society some are guilty but all are responsible" and then ask a simple question: is it generally the responsibility of a democratic society to come to terms with and correct historical wrongs and, specifically, to do so by tilting employment and education systems toward preferential treatment for identified classes of victims? Does the moral imperative justify potential violations of constitutional rights and the imposition of costs on people who were not individually responsible for the historical wrong?

The Supreme Court has since 1978 rejected this logic and prohibited preference as a tool to correct societal discrimination. Although plaintiffs seeking relief from Berkeley, Michigan, Texas, and Harvard claimed their rights were violated, the court disagreed, holding that the "compelling interest" of diversity justifies departures from conventional admissions criteria if certain conditions are met. By shifting away from the moral argument centered on remedying past wrongs, and toward the idea that educational goals require heterogeneity in the student population, the court imposed new evidentiary requirements: institutions would have to prove (or at least argue forcefully enough) that diversity enhances educational outcomes for all students, and that race-neutral alternatives do not accomplish the desired goal.

And herein lies an inverted commons logic. If in the conventional model rational acts by individuals lead to untenable social consequences, here it is the rational action of the collective (e.g., the university) in pursuit of a legitimate social goal, that imposes potentially unfair costs on individuals. This was the crux of a critical exchange during oral

arguments in the *Grutter v. Bollinger* case, which I para-
phrase here:

> MAUREEN MAHONEY (attorney representing the
> University of Michigan): Very few qualified ap-
> plicants would be denied admission under the
> university's race-conscious admissions policy.
> JUSTICE SCALIA: How many does it take before the
> Fourteenth Amendment kicks in?[13]

Having pleaded for not treating commons logic as the last
word, I would apply the same ethic here. There may, indeed,
be a remorselessly unwelcome effect on some individuals of
a social decision to correct historical wrongs and create a
more just system with greater opportunity for disadvantaged
and minoritized citizens. Using the analogy of a driver looking for parking and growing angry because the one vacant
spot is reserved for the disabled, economist and Nobel laureate George Akerlof pointed out that the real difference in
odds of getting into elite institutions because of affirmative
action is asymptotically close to zero. The math is correct,
but whether that would have been enough to sway Justice
Scalia or current members of the court is dubious.

And yet . . . what kinds of creative policy arrangements
or arguments might be devised to justify the advancement of
social benefit? It is worth noting here another civics lesson
embedded in the case, regarding tensions between legal
(constitutional) and social-scientific norms of evidence and
inquiry. Ironically, it was a seasoned attorney (Mahoney) who
made what is essentially an economic benefit/cost argu-

ment; her verbal exchange with Mr. Scalia serves as metaphor for a large class of problems in which the intuitively and theoretically plausible criterion of social benefits exceeding private costs may not pass muster without nontrivial compromises.[14]

Whether the inverted commons model as applied to admissions policies (and the other issues included in this chapter) will open young people's eyes and minds to the complexity of modern democracy, and engage them in pursuit of viable decision strategies, will depend on the capacity and commitment of well-prepared teachers. But even the best teachers cannot solve the problems of civic responsibility and democracy on their own. In the next chapter, I return to the rationale for collaboration between schools and their constituencies.

CHAPTER

4

BEYOND THE
SCHOOLHOUSE
EDUCATION AS PUBLIC GOOD

Education is the province not only of the school but of other agencies as well. The family, institutions of religion, agencies of the state, political groupings, informal as well as formal media of communication, and the general quality of human associations and cultural traditions—all have a part in education.

ISRAEL SCHEFFLER

> Did you teach your teachers enough today,
> or do they expect you back tomorrow?
>
> OTTO FEUER, CIRCA 1961*

HISTORIANS OF AMERICAN SCIENCE generally agree that Vannevar Bush's contribution was transformational. His 1947 report to President Truman laid out a radical vision for the financing and conduct of research post–World War II. Its innovative flair was a new relationship, built on formal and tacit collaborations between government, universities, and the commercial technology sector. Bush, an engineer (no relation to American presidents), reinforced familiar economic principles—comparative advantage and division of labor—in his demarcation of the public and private sectors. His argument—the federal government has to support foundational research because private investors will not risk developing nonexcludable knowledge—was a formulation of what is now taken as basic public goods theory. "Endless Frontier" went a step further, with a convincing logic of partnership: government-funded basic research should be conducted in universities, where academic freedom fuels the engines of discovery, while the commercial sector would translate the fruits of foundational science into marketable technologies. The basic/applied paradigm, and later establishment of the National Science Foundation, propelled American scientific hegemony during much of the twentieth century.[1]

---

* Thanks to my father, of blessed memory, I grew up with an appreciation of the importance of adding my own (and others') experiences to classroom learning. Some of my teachers were okay with that.

The partnership model in "Endless Frontier" has traces in the history and philosophy of public schooling. Like basic science, education produces general knowledge and equips people with skills and dispositions that benefit society as a whole. Although individuals reap private returns from their schooling, general education (as distinct from training in specific skills relevant to specific applications) is very much a social (or public) good, to be financed with public funds. Its value, moreover, is a function of its relevance to the economic and social environment in which the knowledge and skills find application, which necessitates and is nourished by ties between educators and their diverse external communities. Formally and tacitly, public schools in America thrive in mutually reinforcing partnerships with business, government, media, and the arts.[2]

It is unclear whether Vannevar Bush knew the subtleties of American educational philosophy or of the economic theory of public goods and consciously applied them to his views on the respective and connective roles of government, universities, and the private sector. But it is not coincidental that scientific research and education policy share conceptual and organizational attributes. In fact, I would argue that the peculiar genius of the American education system, with its complex and flexible allowances for public and private involvement, served as a proof-point for principles that would later become central to American science. Just as today's great university-based laboratories, funded both from public and private sources, operate under evolving rules for external oversight balanced with safeguards to protect academic independence, public schools have always interacted with government, public interest groups, and private stakeholders. To the extent that concepts of engagement and partnership, politically fraught as they often are, have been essential to the improvement of science, it is worth borrowing from that history to solidify the argument that civic education, too, will benefit from reinforced partnerships between schools and their stakeholders.

Given that school is where principles of citizenship and democracy are supposed to be taught as much by process as by pedagogy, by an interactive blend of doing and didactics, it follows that how schools interact with their constituencies is central to the broad mission of public education. The context for such interactions is, of course, complex. Community engagement consists of a web of formal, legal, and casual arrangements. Parents are encouraged to get involved, and in some cases provide not only intellectual and emotional support but are called upon to raise money for various school activities not covered by the official budget. For perhaps obvious reasons, infusion of cash by more affluent families, whose kids go to "better" schools, raises equity concerns, and for some teachers and principals too much parental engagement is intrusive. In any case, schooling is still understood in most places as something that "takes a village," even if in recent years ideological and religious passions have interfered with healthy, respectful, and mutually supportive deliberation.[3]

Relations between schools and governmental authorities are largely oriented toward the exercise of accountability, a pillar of democratic governance that gained prominence (if not dominance) in education policy over the past half-century. To simplify, because "taxpayers have the right to know" how

their money is spent, American education is awash in requirements for disclosure of everything from what is taught in
classrooms to how much teachers are paid to how well students perform. (Note again, the analogy with science, where
public accountability translates to increasingly demanding
evidence that standards of academic integrity are met and
that the outputs of science add value to humanity.) Especially with the advent of outcomes-based assessment of the
performance and quality of teaching and learning and increased reliance on standardized testing, which (as noted in
chapter 2) coincided with new methods of collecting and reporting data on student achievement (including international
comparative measures), accountability in education has taken
on a ferocity that many researchers and other observers worry
has had unintended and sustaining negative consequences, especially when standardized testing is the accountability tool
of choice.[4]

Without indulging in a long treatise on the benefits and
risks of accountability, the main point here is that decisions regarding content, form, and processes of education—including
curriculum and graduation requirements—are subject to in-
cessant negotiations between school authorities, legislative
bodies of various sorts, local community and parent groups,
and the general public through mainstream and social media.
As I showed earlier, the content of curricula is governed,
with varied specificity and on different schedules, by state education authorities, district offices, and the federal government,
and often involves complex business transactions with private
curriculum and assessment developers. Leaving aside whether
this political-bureaucratic arrangement is healthy, not to men-

tion "optimal," a question hotly debated by policy makers with varied political leanings, it creates a challenge but also an opportunity.

Because schools are inextricably linked to their public and private constituencies, not only does curriculum reform require engagement with the outside world but the process and content of that engagement can be a platform for enriched public discourse on foundational axioms of democratic life. Put simply, it is important to revive the meaning of public education to include education of, with, and for the public. If this is a vulgarized simplification of an essentially Deweyan theory of democracy, so be it. But the practical challenge is to see how these ideals might be made operational. Through what arrangements can civics with the "s" lead to societal civic advancement? Can we learn from the experience of American science—and borrow from its partnership models—to ensure that the proposed revival of civic consciousness is nourished by strong and mutually respectful ties among educators, business leaders, and other influencers? Moreover, is there a case for special attention to international collaboration in the light of growing anxiety about democratic institutions in much of the free world? I turn now to a brief discussion of different types of partnerships that I believe are not only feasible but necessary for the successful revival of civics and civic education.*

---

* As I write this, newspapers are flooded with stories of political intrusions into schooling at all levels, fueled in large part by misunderstandings of concepts such as critical race theory and overcharged edginess about teaching of climate, sexual orientation, gender identity, and reproductive health. Readers will judge if my plea for sanity in relations between schools and their external stakeholders is hopelessly naïve or realistically hopeful.

CAMPUS COMPACTS

Let's start with a recap of the general strategy: to infuse in college and university-based educator preparation a set of principles related to collective action, from which it is hoped that current and future high school teachers will acquire new tools (and new confidence in using them) to engage young people in the tough issues facing democracy today. A relatively straightforward first step should be experimenting with collaborations *within* colleges and universities, aimed at fostering interdisciplinary learning and the spread of lessons from political economy beyond the confines of education departments and schools. Depending on the focus of particular courses and syllabi, faculty from a range of disciplines—in the humanities, social sciences, and professions—could selectively be engaged in innovative co-teaching and/or joint research projects. A word of caution, however: in most institutions of higher education, as in many complex organizations, collaboration is easier to preach than to practice. Departmental budgeting arrangements and tenure criteria, reinforced by the workings of the main disciplinary societies, encourage turf-protection. In what will by now sound like a familiar tune, pursuit of individual or departmental self-interest by rational academics can impede progress toward the social good from enriched cross-program cooperation. University leadership is necessary to provide intellectual support and financial resources to faculty and staff willing to build bridges for civic education across silos of specialization. The process-product dichotomy is relevant here again. The design of jointly taught classes by faculty with diverse academic training and traditions will, in itself, promote new understanding of core issues for future high school teachers, and the resulting syllabi and instructional experiences will become products hopefully with long shelf life.*

Assuming more commitment to interdisciplinary cooperation is feasible, as evidenced by efforts underway in a number of distinguished public and private universities, I offer (in boxes 5 and 6) abridged descriptions of two potential MA-level courses to include in secondary teacher education programs, in hopes of whetting appetites of faculty colleagues to venture out of their departmental comfort zones. In the first such course, the goal would be to introduce basic concepts of private and public goods and externalities in pluralist democracies; the second course, a possible elective for prospective high school STEM teachers, would make explicit the connections between bench science, social responsibility, and the civic good. The significance and subtlety of those connections should not be underestimated: as one reviewer of an earlier draft of this book put it, "We cannot go to Mars unless we have a fundamental understanding of our government!" In both of my curricular "nudges," the baseline hypothesis is that multidisciplinary instruction can add nuance to the preparation of future educators and their ability to include concepts of the civic good in their classroom work. (Faculty names are fictitious.)

---

* Based on years of grappling with the exhortations of staff at the National Academy of Sciences to work across their divisional lines, my colleague Peter Blair coined the phrase "collaboration tax." He may not have known it, but his insight served as a subtle application of what the political economist Mancur Olson (1965) had called "the logic of collective action."

BOX 5. THEORY AND PRACTICE OF COLLECTIVE ACTION
A REQUIRED COURSE FOR SECONDARY SCHOOL TEACHERS

Course description

In this course, students will participate in a jointly taught series of presentations and interactive discussions aimed at acquainting them with fundamentals of "public goods" theory and its relevance to modern pluralist democracy. The goal of the course is to equip future high school teachers with the basic principles of political economy, to be infused in their social studies, American government, economics, and civics classes. Through assigned readings, text study, and group experiential assignments, teacher candidates will gain new perspectives on key challenges to democratic governance, and become more skilled at motivating their current and future pupils to understand fundamental tensions between individual freedom and group consequences.

Faculty (both faculty at each class meeting)

Professor A. Smythe (Economics and public policy)

Professor J. Duey (Education)

Required readings

· G. Hardin, "Tragedy of the Commons," *Science,* 1968

T. Schelling, *Micromotives and Macrobehavior,* 2006, selections

E. Ostrom, "A Behavioral Approach to the Rational Choice Theory of Collective Action," 1997

Class meetings and assignments (biweekly, four hours)

Introduction of faculty and students and overview of course expectations (*Smythe, Duey*)

- Theory of "the commons" (*Smythe*)
- Commons logic in common schools (*Duey*)
- Student team presentations: Based on visit to partnering high school, what are preliminary impressions of opportunities and obstacles to engaging young learners in discussions of choice, values, and outcomes?

From general principles to specific examples (*Smythe*)

- Environment (externalities and how to manage them)
- Congestion (choice, consequences, and potential "solutions")

From theory to pedagogy (*Duey*)

- How to teach externalities
- How to teach social choice
- Prisoner's Dilemma and implications (*Smythe*)

Student team presentations (part two)

Reports from the field: experiments in high school civics classes

BOX 6. TEACHING SCIENCE AND SCIENCE POLICY

A REQUIRED COURSE FOR SECONDARY SCHOOLTEACHERS

Course description

In this course, students will develop a skill set relevant to enriching high school STEM classes with issues in science policy. The goal is to prepare future teachers to engage all students—whether they plan to go into science and mathematics or other non-STEM fields—in basic aspects of the financing, organization, politics, and ethics of scientific research. Through assigned readings, text study, and group experiential assignments, students will gain new perspectives on key tensions at the intersection of scientific method and democratic governance.

Faculty (all faculty at each class meeting)

Professor R. Atkins (Science policy)

Professor B. Albert (Science education)

Professor H. Basse (Mathematics education)

Required readings

V. Bush, "Science: The Endless Frontier," 1947

Next Generation Science Standards at https://www.nextgenscience.org/

National Council of Teachers of Mathematics at https://www.nctm.org/standards/

Class meetings and assignments (biweekly, four hours)

Introduction and overview of course expectations

American science since World War II (*Atkins*)

- How good are science and math education? (*Albert, Basse*)

- Student team presentations (part one): Based on visit to partnering high school, what are preliminary impressions of opportunities and obstacles to engaging young learners in discussions of science and mathematics as public goods?

From general principles to specific examples: Science (*Albert*)

- Biology and human genetics
- Chemistry and climate

> From general principles to specific examples: Math (*Basse*)
> • Mathematics of voting
> • Mathematics of social justice
> Financing and management of government, philanthropy, ethics (*Atkins*)
> Student team presentations (part two): Reports from the field: how receptive are high school students to science as a public good?

A WIDER CIRCLE

Seasoned college administrators and faculty may find the notion of cross-campus collaboration quaint, if not whimsical in the way many of them often view the prospect of serving as volunteers on interdisciplinary National Academies committees. Based on my experience, though, most academics come around to seeing the virtues of such activity, and I believe that if faculty from the STEM and humanities disciplines can be persuaded (and offered incentives) to work with faculty in departments and schools of education, the result will be mutually beneficial and downright pleasant. It is a type of partnership that should be explored and tried (and given that students in many colleges and universities already take courses across the wide offerings on their campuses, the idea that their faculty might go along for the ride seems all the more realistic).

Perhaps simultaneously, the collaborations suggested here could be embellished with partners from the outside. Four possibilities come to mind. First, and perhaps most simply, teacher educators involved with campus colleagues in courses of the type outlined in boxes 5 and 6 could invite guests from "the real world" to join some or all of the class sessions. For example, in the class focused on environmental policy and externalities, why not have a panel of experts from the US Environmental Protection Agency, the American Chemical Society, and the World Wildlife Fund—and rebuttals from the Cato or American Enterprise Institutes? Similarly, in the class on congestion and the analytics of individually rational choice that leads to phenomena such as rubbernecking, it would add real-world value to include experts from a state police department, the American Automobile Association, and the local department of motor vehicles. (When I taught that story, having a distinguished engineer as a respondent added considerably to the conversation.) For the STEM policy course, ideal outsiders would include senior officials of the National Science Foundation or National Institutes of Health; experts from one or more foundations that support scientific research such as the Howard Hughes Medical Institute or the Moore Foundation; an executive from the National Academy of Sciences; the head of the Center for Science in the Public Interest or similar organization concerned with ethics; and someone from "big pharma" to explain the views and challenges of the private sector in funding and managing research. To the extent that many faculty already issue such invitations to enrich their classes, it should not be hard to apply the model to discussions on civics and civic responsibility.

If these strategies seem ad hoc, more formal arrangements would be worth developing, again focused on collaborations between teacher educators, their university colleagues, and influential organizations outside academe. An example is to establish a sustained activity under the aegis of the National Academy of Education. Something like a "board on civics, science, and education" could be the catalyst for a wide range of processes and products including workshops on the issues covered in teacher prep classes involving stakeholders representing various perspectives and political leanings; consensus panels charged with exploring research and evidence on the effectiveness of new curricula and pedagogies; organized interactions with government officials and staff, editorial boards, social media entrepreneurs, and local community organizers; and regular (perhaps annual) audits of the condition of civics education, using National Assessment and other useful data. Borrowing from the important reviews of scientific disciplines regularly undertaken by various academies, a national report on the status of civics curriculum and pedagogy would advance the cause.

A variation on that approach would be to adapt the successful Government-University-Industry Research Roundtable (known as GUIRR), a long-standing activity of the National Academies of Sciences, Engineering, and Medicine (NASEM). GUIRR is "charged with improving the research enterprise of the United States by successfully resolving the cross-sectoral issues that prevent the U.S. research enterprise from reaching its full potential. This mission is achieved by convening senior-most representatives from government, universities, and industry to frame the critical issues, followed—when appropriate—by the execution of activities designed to address specific cross-sectoral impediments to achieving a healthy, vibrant research enterprise." Unlike other NASEM activities that produce consensus reports with recommendations, GUIRR's contributions are largely based on *process*: bringing together disparate and divergent voices representing sector-specific expertise in the hope of encouraging mutual learning and potential collaboration. By extension, a similar process-oriented entity, under the leadership of the National Academy of Education, could advance civic understanding and the preparation of future teachers with robust deliberations of school-based and external stakeholders. Such an activity would need support, financial and moral, from relevant federal agencies (e.g., the Institute for Education Sciences and the National Science Foundation) as well as private foundations concerned with the preservation of democratic norms.

A fourth addition to the menu of potential innovations would be to develop a set of research-practice partnerships (RPPs) connecting political economy researchers who study the dynamics of choice and consequences with school districts eager to infuse new ideas in their civics curricula, and to report on the successes (and failures) of such experiments to enable possible imitation and emulation in other locales. The literature on such partnerships already provides important clues to why and how such engagements can be designed and implemented effectively.[5]

Finally, and more ambitiously, I would encourage cross-national partnerships, for example between the NASEM/NAEd, OECD, the World Bank, and other nongovernmental organizations working in the developed and developing world on the strengthening of civic responsibility and democracy, in general and in education specifically. In this arena, improvement of the design, implementation, interpretation, and uses of international comparative assessment data would be a welcome benefit. Using comparative testing not only to produce high-stakes rankings that have proven in some cases to distract governments from developing informed policy but to promote cooperation in design of new civics-oriented curricula would be highly desirable. Such a strategy could lead toward greater global cooperation not just on mutual understanding of student learning of civics and the preparation and quality of their teaching forces but could foster needed collaboration on problems of climate, pandemic treatment, conflict resolution, and other public goods that do not honor sovereign boundaries.

There are numerous financial and organizational obstacles that need to be overcome in the design and launch of international partnerships and sustainable collaborations. I would start small therefore—say, with a project involving policy analysts and scientists from two countries. Rather than convene one-off conferences, I would explore the possibility for a sustained engagement leading to a set of products such as joint working papers, a digital platform for data sharing, and gatherings with policy makers and other influencers in both countries. Two examples come to mind, namely Azerbaijan and Israel, countries committed to advancement of human capital and reduction of economic inequality and involved in complex deliberations over definitions of pluralism, national identity, citizenship, and security. My experience working in those places gives me confidence that such engagements would be feasible, mutually beneficial, and instructive to others interested in global cooperation on the preservation of democracy.[6]

The theories of collective action at the heart of this book, relating to the problems of individual self-interest and the social good, should serve as a cautionary reminder that rhetoric in support of collaboration is often insufficient without funding to overcome constraints faced by any of the potential participants to foot the bill. There are already a number of philanthropies experienced in global cooperation that could be called upon for support of a new global civic education initiative. The public returns on such investment could be significant, in terms of the generalizability of the knowledge about how to manage partnerships, and in terms of the utility of emergent findings for curriculum developers and educators everywhere. I hope this book might be part of the kindling to ignite such a process.

POSTSCRIPT

"COMMONS" SENSE IN DEMOCRATIC EDUCATION

A COLLECTIVE PROJECT FOR THE COLLECTIVE GOOD

IN MY BOOK ABOUT PHILANTHROPY and public policy (*The Rising Price of Objectivity*), which celebrated the remarkable growth of independent think tanks and what I called "the advice industry," I mused that "Americans flirt with stupidity, but they buy knowledge." Pithy? Yes, but obvious misplaced optimism given that the book appeared in November 2016, about a month after a presidential campaign operative announced that "People that say that facts are facts—they're not really facts . . . there's no such thing, unfortunately." A lesson from that experience is that the time between drafting a final manuscript and seeing a book in print is often enough to render at least some of its punditry and prognostications too dated to be useful. In the case of America's struggle to preserve democracy, I have no doubt that I will have missed or misunderstood the significance of rapidly changing events, positive and negative. So this postscript is in part a preemptive apology. Too much is in flux to attempt a comprehensive update, but some last-minute contextual reminders are worth trying.

As I write, the nation is girding itself for what promises to be another brutalizing round of voting frenzy, polluted by outrageous conspiracy theories regarding the validity of election results, malicious exploitation of racial rhetoric, persistent substitution of pluralism with a nasty strain of divisionalism, more climate catastrophes around the world, and relentless transformation of healthy partisanship into mean-spirited and vile rhetoric. I could reference a seemingly limitless sounding of alarms about our precarious position. In the November 6, 2022, Sunday *New York Times*, for example, the editorial board opined that "political violence is threatening our democracy." Suffice it to say there is enough going on to lure me into answering my optimism-pessimism riddle with resigned negativity—sadly, the data are dismal.

On the other hand, or shall I say on the other page, the same issue of the Sunday *Times* reported on an effort by the "New Pluralists." With generous philanthropic support, about $100 million as of November 2022, this group has been working on an experiment aimed at fixing what for readers of this book will sound like a familiar diagnosis: "Too many Americans lack the skills, the opportunity and even the inclination to work together despite their differences toward a common goal." (The word "common" is becoming more commonplace even as threats to the common good are becoming more, well, common.) In terms of public resilience that sometimes defies conventional predictions, the 2022 midterm elections resulted in reminders of the surprise factor in American politics: as one astute and honest commentator noted, "Yesterday was a good day for democracy. Some of the worst election deniers and kookiest candidates were sent packing, in many cases by larger margins than anyone— including me—expected."[1]

These examples are soothing and reinforce my hope that there are at least reasonably good chances enough Americans will come to their senses, that the culture of community responsibility and caring will prevail, that we will see a return to sanity in the workings of government, and that this year's (and presumably next year's) threats to democracy will be quashed the way earlier ones were in the nineteenth and twentieth centuries. On the optimism-pessimism spectrum, I continue to see evidence of our nation's broad and deep-seated resolve to heed Benjamin Franklin's admonition to "keep" our republic. And I remain perhaps immodestly (if not irrationally) enthusiastic for a book about the *long-term* value of imbuing in civic education concepts and principles about the "common good." Hence, the volume in your hands (in print or on your e-reader).

I have concentrated here on one fault line in our democratic geology, namely the vexing tensions between the virtues of individual freedom and the hazards of social calamity. And I have proposed a way to instill more knowledge and sensitivity about those issues—which fit broadly under the rubric of the "tragedy of the commons"—simultaneously in the hearts and minds of professionals who prepare future educators, working teachers and their constituents, and the complex external ecology of business, philanthropy, and government.[2]

It will, indeed, take at least that kind of concerted effort to make a difference, and I grow more confident knowing that others are working assiduously on other components of civic behavior—namely, youth engagement with social issues, reform of voting and rules of election financing and participation, and the host of skills that are essential to the meanings of citizenship in a complex pluralist and moral democracy. Most important, regardless of short-term disruptions and on the assumption that our basic institutions will stand, keeping concepts of rights and results prominent in civic education should be a commitment for the long run.

Ah, *the long run*. It's hard to not allude here to another great economist, Lord Keynes, famous for his warning that "in the long run we're all dead." Perhaps misunderstood by noneconomists, this turn of phrase was and remains a reminder that prospects for a more hopeful future hinge to a great degree on our willingness and ability to do things now, even if no single short-term act is likely to fix the bigger mess or guarantee a perfectly desirable and sustainable outcome. Balancing the treatment of short-term emergencies with a steady eye on the long term is a challenge that policy makers often fail to confront properly. If one accepts the baseline assumption motivating this book—that the long-run safety of democracy hinges in part on appreciation by the citizenry of tensions between individual rights and social outcomes and how to navigate them—then now is a good time to experiment at the local level, even with incomplete, imperfect, and not fully tested interventions, as we keep the distant future in mind.[3]

Where to start? My argument has centered on the perhaps familiar refrain that to reinforce the foundations and infrastructure of our complex democracy, investment in education—in and out of schools—should be among our highest priorities. I say this confident in the resiliency of the school system to adopt curricular reforms that promote engagement with the diverse interests that surround (and rely on) our complicated education system. The current environment may not seem hospitable to the respectful discourse needed to advance civic knowledge and engagement, which is why it's important to keep these ideas on a shelf of long life; still, acceptance of some delay in gratification will be important.

One way to approach the task, I have suggested, is to rethink how we prepare future educators, those brave souls who aspire to work not only in school classrooms but in think tanks and corporate board rooms and foundations and media conglomerates and human resources offices. The logic is that by infusing into university-based teacher education programs an enriched dose of theory and experiential evidence regarding fundamentals of choice, markets, and public goods, we stand a chance of influencing educators whose work brings them into daily contact with the messiness of "moral democracy" and whose influence on future generations of decision makers and leaders is powerful. As a not inconsequential side benefit, revising the education school curriculum in the way I am proposing will itself enable and encourage new and productive collaborations among scholars and practitioners who don't typically perceive incentives for the kind of collective action needed to overcome the failures of rational self-interest seeking.

Thinking about education reform as *process* and *product*, the subtleties of private incentives colliding with desirable public consequences need to be addressed not only through enriched pedagogy but as much by reform in basic organizational structures that promote experiential learning. Learning-by-doing is nowhere as crucial as in the realm of civics and civic well-being. At risk of sounding preachy, it's time to move beyond the rhetoric of cross-campus collaboration and community engagement, and experiment with models that actually promote collective teaching and learning—within colleges and universities and in partnerships with schools and business and government and media leaders on the outside.

I began this book (and titled it) with a question: *Can schools save democracy?* Borrowing from another gem of Jewish humor, my answer is . . . another question: *Can we afford to not try?*

ACKNOWLEDGMENTS

★ ★ ★

Colleagues, friends, and family listened patiently to my ideas for this book, read various drafts of some or all of the chapters, and offered wise comments. Early on, Elizabeth Rich helped me untangle the knot of connections between the K–12 and postsecondary sectors, which led me to try the idea of emphasizing teacher education as a main point of leverage in the proposed strategy. Mike Usdan reinforced that idea and offered additional insights and encouragement. Chip Edelsberg, Amy Berman, Ellen Lagemann, Mike McPherson, and Anand Desai read drafts and provided enlightened suggestions, too nuanced to catalog or summarize here; for their wisdom and friendship, I will always be indebted. Caroline Chauncey, with her fine eye and ear for the education zeitgeist, enriched my thinking and helped unwrinkle my writing. Dick Atkinson, a cherished friend and mentor, reads most of what I produce and here again tried to keep me balanced and on point. Carl Kaestle, of blessed memory, knew I was working on this, and I only wish his illness had not prevented us from sipping Manhattans and talking through the basic arguments. Sallai Meridor and Avital Darmon helped me think more clearly (as they often do!) about civics generally and the situation in Israel, where educators and policy leaders are steeped in debates over fulfilling aspirations for social justice and educational improvement. I was fortunate to present pieces of the argument at meetings of the Israel Academy of Sciences and Humanities; thanks to Renana Amir, Hanan Alexander, Rami Benbenishti, and others.

Henry Braun read and commented on parts of an early draft and kindly invited me to give the Boisi Lecture at Boston College, where I benefited from the knowledge and instincts of Stanton Wortham, Mike Russell, Marilyn Cochran-Smith, Larry Ludlow, and others. Special thanks to Ida Lawrence for inviting me to speak at ETS, and to Laura Hamilton, Mary Pitoniak, Randy Bennett, and other current or former members of the research and development group there for their astute comments. I benefited from the wit and wisdom of LaVerne Srinivasan, whose own work on education and the common good is making a marked difference. Andy Rotherham, a leader in the struggle for educational progress, was generous with his ideas about curriculum reform and state policy. Stacie Cherner was kind enough to hear me summarize key ideas, and then had me try them out with a group of fellow philanthropists, which led to new discovery and new thinking. I have been a fan and admirer of Lorraine McDonnell for decades, and again she came through with invaluable advice to sharpen the logic and deepen the foundations of my arguments about schooling and public policy. Suzanne Wilson, Bob Floden, Susan Moore-Johnson, James Banks, Judith Torney-Purta, Walter Parker, Peter Levine, Joe

Kahne, Ira Lit, Raj Vinnekota, Adam Gamoran, and Diana Hess were generous with time and knowledge, steering me toward the right data and helping me try to get the data right. Steve Hoffman tried (again) to nudge me from theory to practical applications. Ericka Miller, a cherished friend and damned good coach, listened to my ideas and encouraged me to persist even with all the other obligations on my plate.

My former GW colleague Professor Maia Sheppard, now at the University of Iowa, graciously shared the syllabus she had developed for her secondary social studies teacher preparation course. I also thank Jane Lo, of Michigan State University, and Tom Owenby, of the University of Wisconsin–Madison, for letting me see and learn from their syllabi; and Stanford dean Dan Schwartz for connecting me with his colleague Victor Lee, who quickly sent me and then spoke to me about his fascinating course called "Teaching Data Science in Secondary School." Paul Socken kindly helped me track down Talmudic resources on early Jewish education.

My beloved colleague at GW, Ben Jacobs, an accomplished historian of education, the social studies, and Jewish affairs, offered especially helpful insights. He and Professor Barry Chazan, a dear friend, welcomed me to their class in the Israel Education Program, which gave me yet another chance to spin my story before a group of very civic-minded professionals. Thanks also to Yael Hess, Ido Barkan, and Yonatan Schiff for inviting me to speak on this topic to fellows of the Mandel Leadership Institute in Jerusalem, and to Shelley Kedar for introducing me to a leadership group of the Jewish Agency. My friend and teacher, Rabbi Dan Zemel, offered helpful comments at early stages of the project, as did Peter Dougherty and Jayne Fargnoli. For the extraordinary research assistance of GW doctoral student and educator Amanda Baker, I will always be grateful. Meg Holland has been an indispensable and inspiring colleague, friend, and confidante, always willing to listen to my rants—and counter with subtle questions—on a range of topics.

I have been fortunate to work with and receive wonderful encouragement from Greg Britton and Barbara Kline Pope at Johns Hopkins University Press, from an anonymous reviewer whom I wish I could thank personally, and from Adriahna Conway, Alena Jones, Bea Jackson, and Julie McCarthy for expert version control, literary judgment, and copyediting. Extra thanks to Helen Wheeler and Lunaea Weatherstone at Westchester Publishing Services for superb help with manuscript preparation. Deep gratitude to my agent, Joelle Delbourgo, whose fine antennae and literary sensibilities helped me think about how to reach diverse readers.

Finally, a great big hug and thank-you to my family, for encouraging me and giving me the space and time for this project, which for perhaps obvious reasons had me working on holidays, weekends, and at weird hours of the night.

Introduction. Education and Democracy

1. Since his earlier work, Putnam has continued to plumb the problems of social capital and the civic good, with a perhaps more optimistic view of prospects for renewal. See Putnam 1995, 2000, 2020. The General Social Survey (GSS) is a project of the independent research organization NORC at the University of Chicago, with principal funding from the National Science Foundation; see https://gss.norc.org/. For definitions of social capital, see Claridge 2004.

2. Goldberg 2020; Lozada 2020. Barton Gellman's numerous articles can be found at https://www.theatlantic.com/author/barton-gellman/. Similarly for George Packer, here: https://www.theatlantic.com/author/george-packer/. For an especially interesting commentary about the fragility of democracy, using a "Hirschmanian" framework, see Lozada 2022.

3. For a compelling analysis of the deterioration of the Republican Party and its impacts on civil discourse, see Milbank 2022.

4. Landwehr and Schäfer 2020; Rai and Wible 2020; Snyder 2017; Applebaum 2020. The situation in Israel has dedicated Zionists, Jews and non-Jews, the world over, spanning the political spectrum except for fringes of extremism on left and

right, concerned for the moral and economic fabric of the Jewish state and its historical commitment to democracy and equality. For commentary see, e.g., Berman, Peretz, Walzer, and Wieseltier 2023; Oren 2023; and Harari 2023. Similar judicial reforms in Mexico have spurred repeated and massive protests. See Graham 2023.

5. For analysis of antiracist protests after George Floyd, see Buchanan, Bui, and Patel 2020. Galston is quoted in the summary by Rucker et al. 2020. See also Kamarck 2021; Dionne 2021.

6. Lemann 1996; Fallows and Fallows 2018.

7. Gamoran et al. 2021.

8. Lapin 2021. See also Rachel Maddow's podcast *Ultra*, which offers reminders of other evil characters in the drama of American history.

9. For the difference between "clinching" and "vouching for" claims, see Cartwright 2011.

10. Students of early twentieth-century history know that some of the worst tyrants rose to power through processes that claimed to adhere to at least some version of democratic procedure. "Moral democracy," then, borrowed from Carugati and Levi 2021, is a way of conditioning superficially democratic processes, an apt reminder that majority voting systems, for example, may not produce morally acceptable outcomes.

11. The phrase "tragedy of the commons" entered popular discourse with Hardin 1968.

12. On the role of education in democracy, perhaps the best source is McDonnell, Timpane, and Benjamin 2000. For a good example of excessive blaming of schools for various social and economic problems, see Klein, Rice, and Levy 2012. For a moderated view, see Feuer 2012. For a recent and thoughtful argument about the role of universities in democracy, see Daniels 2021.

13. Against my assertion that regulated capitalism has done the most to improve economic and social opportunities, some may offer the Chinese economic miracle and that country's success in bringing millions of people out of poverty as a counterfactual. But to suggest that China is an example of regulated *democratic* capitalism requires more than a stretch of imagination. See Schuman 2022.

14. See Kaestle 2000. The argument that civics and STEM could be mutually reinforcing is in Feuer 2021b.

15. For the meaning of "pedagogical content knowledge," one of Lee Shulman's enduring contributions to education theory and practice, see Gudmundsdottir and Shulman 1987.

1. Free to Bruise

1. Data on religious practices in the United States are drawn from the "Religious Landscapes Study," Pew Research Center, Washington, D.C., 2014. For additional information regarding the complexity of American religious practice, see Greeley and Hout 2006. As noted in an astute commentary comparing trends in the United States and Israel, "Recent decades have seen a dramatic decline in Christian identification in the United States, while traditional Jewish practice in Israel has ticked upward." See Willick 2023 and Pew Research Center 2022. A more chilling portrayal of American religiosity and its effects on politics comes from recent polling by the Public Religion Research Institute: see "A Christian Nation? Understanding the Threat of Christian Nationalism to American Democracy and Culture," 2023.

2. How and why this meaning of conservatism became displaced by a nasty strain of antichoice authoritarianism is beyond my scope but adds an important dimension to the already complex context for civic education. For a recent analysis with emphasis on trends in the Republican party, see Milbank 2022.

3. One need only think of Joseph McCarthy, Jesse Helms, Newt Gingrich, Lindsey Graham, Ilhan Omar, or Marjorie Taylor Greene to appreciate how maintaining any semblance of a moderate center has always been a challenge. The "dance of legislation" was the title of Eric Redman's wonderful 1973 analysis of congressional politics (see Redman 2000). I am grateful to an anonymous reviewer of an earlier draft of this book for the reminder that there is also a "dance of administration," i.e., that our complex system actually has four branches. On Americans' faith in the Social Security system, see Public Policy Polling 2016. As far as anomalies go, the fact that environmental protection as a government priority was the brainchild of Richard Nixon ranks high. See Lewis 1985.

4. For the verbatim words of Senator Romney and the rebuttal by Martin Luther King III, see Romney 2022; and King 2021.

5. See Feuer 1984 for the example of state liquor stores in the broader context of bureaucratic overrreach.

6. On the US standard of living compared to other countries, see World Population Review 2023. For discussion of American trends in higher education compared to other countries, see Feuer 2012; and Goldin and Katz 2008. On the growth and significance of think tanks, see Feuer 2016. Where we stand on indexes of economic inequality is documented in Hauser 2020. For recent analysis of higher education in the context of economic and demographic inequality, see Baum and McPherson 2022.

7. Compulsory education has roots in early rabbinic teaching. See, e.g., Socken 2022; and Sacks 2004. See also the William Davidson Talmud, *Nedarim 81a*, translated by Koren-Steinsaltz, available at https://www.sefaria.org/Nedarim.81a.3/. Conant is quoted in Boorstin 1973.

8. According to PDK International, "Despite the challenges of
the pandemic, Americans continue to have high opinions
of their local schools and teachers in particular. Similarly,
respondents are highly confident overall in their local school's
ability to handle potential challenges in the new school year."
See https://pdkpoll.org/. But there is compelling evidence
of discord too: recent survey work by Grinnell College
revealed that on particular issues such as racial history and
affirmative action "a majority of Americans thinks public
schools are on the wrong track." See https://www.grinnell
.edu/news/grinnell-poll-education-march-22. For analysis of
trends in public and private school enrollments, see Murnane
and Reardon 2018.

9. On American philanthropy, see Feuer 2016; Feuer 2021a;
and Lagemann 1989. Compelling arguments about the value
of philanthropy in democracy are in Brest and Harvey 2018.
The notion of "contestatory" aspects of philanthropy was
introduced by Reich 2013.

10. The preeminent social demographer Sam Preston and
colleagues analyzed American longevity (life expectancy
compared to other countries). See Crimmins, Preston, and
Cohen 2011; also see Tierney 2009. The Institute of
Medicine report is accessible at https://nap.nationalacademies
.org/catalog/10188/coverage-matters-insurance-and
-health-care. For recent work on the effects of health
insurance and other factors explaining health outcomes,
see Robert Wood Johnson Foundation 2014; and James
House 2015. On disparities in health care, see also Feuer
2018.

11. "Rival views" is aptly in the title of one of Albert Hirschman's
seminal books. See Hirschman 1992. "Nudge" became a
social scientific term thanks to behavioral economists Richard
Thaler and Cass Sunstein (2009).

12. See Berlin 1997; and Lilla, Dworkin, and Silvers 2001. For the logic of "externalities," see, e.g., Moffatt 2019. For application to education, see Feuer 2010. On property rights and market solutions to externalities, see Coase 2013.

13. See Friedman and Friedman 1980; and Hayek 1969. For critique of economists with conservative leanings, see Romer 2020; and my rebuttal in Feuer 2020b. I am grateful to Amy Berman for the reminder that "political uptake" may not be an apt metaphor for how things worked under the dictatorial Pinochet regime. My main point, though, is to remember that there is often a "demand side" in politics that influences and reinforces economists' input.

14. Smith, *Wealth of Nations* (2003 edition); and *The Theory of Moral Sentiments* (1971 edition). See economics Nobel laureate Amartya Sen's reminder of Smith's own beliefs on the limits of markets (*New York Times* 2022).

15. The classic exposition of positive economics is in Friedman 1966; see also Lipsey 1971. Examples of texts in mathematical economics include Henderson and Quandt 1958; Samuelson 1955; Stiglitz 1997; and Krugman and Wells 2015. Albert Hirschman's work stands out in twentieth-century literature challenging purist market dogma. See Adelman 2013; and Lozada 2022. For an enlightened perspective on the virtues and limits of markets in the context of technological progress, see Baumol 2002.

16. Voltaire's warning to not let perfection be the enemy of good (often misstated as "enemy of *the* good") was first published in his *Dictionnaire philosophique* and later made it into a poem he wrote, *La Bégueule*. For the pathbreaking work of Herbert Simon, see Lindbeck 1992; and *Encyclopedia Britannica* 2023. On the application of principles of bounded and procedural rationality to economic organization, see Williamson 1975; and Augier and March 2004. The advent of "behavioral economics" associated with, for example, Daniel Kahn-

emann and Amos Twersky can be traced to the earlier work of Simon et al. Surprisingly, that connection was and remains largely neglected in popular writing (see, e.g., Lewis 2017). For a particularly innovative set of applications of behavioral economics to explaining policy success and failure, see List 2022.

17. For compelling analysis of unnecessary deaths from COVID-19 due to policy failure, see the work of Jeff Shaman and colleagues at Columbia University, summarized by Glanz and Robertson 2020. See also Feuer 2020c and 2021c; and Remnick 2020.

18. Charles Lindblom's discussion of Soviet-era central planning is classic: see his *Politics and Markets* 1980.

19. For Dr. Fauci's rebuttal of Dr. Paul, see https://www.cnn .com/videos/politics/2022/01/11/dr-anthony-fauci-rand -paul-coronavirus-hearing-vpx.cnn.

20. "Prisoner's Dilemma," *Stanford Encyclopedia of Philosophy*, https://plato.stanford.edu/entries/prisoner-dilemma/. For application to the COVID-19 pandemic, see Roberts 2020.

21. Hardin (1968) has been cited and referenced thousands of times in the years since the publication of his article in *Science*. A recent Google search for "tragedy of the commons" yielded more than 80,000 results.

22. See Arrow 1963. For discussion, see "Arrow's Theorem," *Stanford Encyclopedia of Philosophy*, https://plato.stanford.edu /entries/arrows-theorem/.

23. For the debate over welfare reform, see Murray and Jencks 1985 and Hirschman 1991. On the situation in special education, I am grateful to Beth Tuckwiller; see Fitzgerald and Watkins 2006. See also Lozada 2022.

24. The evidence of delay in American response to news of the Nazi holocaust is chilling. Still, when the decision was taken to go to war, the overwhelming majority of Americans answered the call. To understand why and how today's youth

are fed up with adult excuses about climate change and other environmental catastrophes, see, e.g., Thunberg 2019.

2. Civics as Process and Product

1. See Walzer 2004. I am grateful to Stanford professor Ira Lit for the phrase "civic orientation." Another work from which I borrowed here is *Educating the Democratic Mind* (Parker 1996), which includes essays by Newmann et al. and Angell and Hahn. On policy borrowing, see, e.g., Williams and Engel 2013; and Phillips and Ochs 2003. For a perspective on the history of pluralism in the United States, see Mendes-Flohr 2022. As noted earlier, compulsory education has roots in early rabbinic teaching. Jeff Mirel's last book before his untimely and tragic death, *Patriotic Pluralism*, is essential: see Mirel 2010.

2. Elmore (who tragically passed away in 2021) made the comment at a meeting at the National Research Council. In *Politics and Markets*, Charles Lindblom offered the memorable imagery of state systems with strong thumbs . . . and weak fingers (Lindblom 1980). I cautioned in my book on rationality in education that innovative benefits accrued from local control need to be weighed against the egregious harms of school segregation and other locally preferred policies. See Feuer 2006, which applies Herbert Simon's theories of decision making, e.g., Simon 1978. Hirschman's "possibilism" is especially useful in considering models of rationality; see Ferraton and Frobert 2017.

3. See Newmann et al., "Skills in Citizen Action," in Parker 1996. On the value of argumentation in policy making, see Feuer 2022. On consensus as a form of knowledge production, see Feuer and Maranto 2010.

4. Parker 1996.

5. Nelson 1994. See also Reuben 1997; and Barr, Barth, and Shermis 1977.

6. See Schneider 1994. See also Adler 2010; and "College, Career, and Civic Life (C3) Framework for Social Studies State Standards," https://www.socialstudies.org/standards/c3.

7. My use of the product/process metaphor will be familiar to students of Herbert Simon (see Simon 1978). For discussion of education not as an end but rather as the means to continued learning, growth, and human development, see Phillips 2016; also Alexander 2015.

8. Niemi and Junn 1998. The story about National Geographic is told in Cremin 1990. For NAEP, see, e.g., National Assessment of Educational Progress (NAEP), 2022 NAEP Report Card: Civics, https://www.nationsreportcard.gov/civics/results/achievement/. For more on the importance of considering variance in performance and its downward-forcing effects on population-wide mean or average academic performance, see Hauser 2020.

9. For rigorous analysis of international implications of national assessment, see Judith Torney-Purta et al. 2021; and on methodological problems with international comparisons, see Braun and Singer 2018. The temptation to use large-scale testing methods to reinforce civics and citizenship is problematic. See, e.g., Carrasco 2022.

10. The quotation about nuance is from Niemi and Junn 1998, fn. 11. Test-based accountability has proven to be a hazardous venture; see Elliott and Hout 2011.

11. Although the statement is often attributed to Lincoln, it most likely was borrowed from a poem by Ella Wheeler Wilcox. See "Reform," in the Project Gutenberg compilation of poems, https://www.gutenberg.org/files/6617/6617-h/6617-h.htm#page92.

12. The best recent work on this subject is Hess and McAvoy 2015.

13. See Hochschild and Scovronick 2003.

14. See Kitcher 2022; also see Crittenden and Levine 2018.
15. A good source for the history and philosophy of NAEP and Ralph Tyler's seminal contribution is "From the NAEP Primer: A Technical History of NAEP," available at https://nces.ed.gov/nationsreportcard/about/newnaephistory.aspx. See also Jones and Olkin 2004; and Mullis 2019.
16. Kaestle 2000. For a discussion of overwrought interpretations of early international test score data, see Feuer 2012 and 2013.
17. The National Council for the Social Studies has argued forcefully about the decline of civics; see https://www.socialstudies.org/news/ncss-responds-assault-democracy. More recent trends, in the wake of the COVID-19 pandemic, are documented in Diliberti, Woo, and Kaufman 2023.

3. Curriculum Options
1. Cremin 1990, 17.
2. Excerpts of requirements in Pennsylvania and Wisconsin are from "Education Commission of the States: 50-State Comparison," Civic Education Policies: High School Graduation Requirements, December 2016. Reference to the Tufts University data is from CIRCLE: Center for Information and Research on Civic Learning and Engagement. Accessible at https://circle.tufts.edu/.
3. For data on Advanced Placement see https://reports.collegeboard.org/ap-program-results. I am grateful to colleagues at ETS for their insights about possibilities for individualization and personalization in AP art assessment.
4. Lee Shulman's contributions to the theory of pedagogy are legendary. See Shulman 1986; and Cochran 1997. For analysis of the diversity of teacher preparation programs in the United States, see, e.g., Feuer et al. 2013.

5. See Lesh 2011; Rubin 2011; Swan, Lee, and Grant 2011; Hess and MacAvoy 2014. With thanks to Maia Shepard, Victor Lee, Tom Owenby, and Jennifer Lo for generous sharing of syllabi.

6. For a recent editorial on integrating civics and science, see Feuer 2021b. For a contemplation of the drift from "objectivity" in mainstream and social media, see Greenberg 2022. On civics in science classes, see Eastern Michigan University 2006. See also Next Generation Science Standards (n.d.).

7. For analysis of the effects of choice on residential and school resegregation, see Rotberg and Glazer 2018. The overarching question, whether improvement of public education is more likely through market mechanisms (choice, vouchers, etc.) or through investments in traditional schools, would be enriched by application of Albert Hirschman's "exit-voice-loyalty" framework; see Hirschman 1970.

8. For historical analysis, see Ravitch 1974; and Kahlenberg 2007.

9. See *New York Times* 2022.

10. See Mufson 2021. For explanation of the basic economics, see Nordhaus 2021.

11. For succinct overviews of the history of affirmative action, see Infoplease, "Timeline of Affirmative Action Milestones," https://www.infoplease.com/history/us/timeline-of-affirmative-action-milestones; Kramer 2019; and Liptak and Hartocollis 2022.

12. The 6–3 ruling of the court was generally seen as ending affirmative action in college admissions, although analysts noted the complexity of the decision and the likelihood that it would lead to considerable new litigation as universities balance their aspirations for diversity with new legal restrictions. See, e.g., Lopez 2023; Wagner et al. 2023. For the full text of the decision, see https://www.supremecourt.gov/opinions/22pdf/20-1199_hgdj.pdf?ftag=MSF0951a18.

13. Justice Ketanji Brown Jackson's interrogation of the lawyer representing the University of North Carolina in the October 2022 case offered a brilliant reframing of the equal protection conundrum. She argued that because personal statements by applicants frequently include direct and indirect references to their race or skin color, prohibiting attention to those attributes only for Black (or other minority) applicants would violate their equal protection rights. It is worth noting also that Justice Sonia Sotomayor's questioning relied heavily on the amicus brief prepared by Amy Berman, Kenji Hakuta, Michal Kurlaender, and Yelena Konanov for the National Academy of Education. See National Academy of Education 2022.

14. The literature on the moral basis for preferential treatment includes work by distinguished jurists as well as philosophers and economists. See, e.g., Dworkin 1998. A landmark economic and institutional analysis is in Bowen and Bok 2000. Akerlof's handicapped-parking analogy appears there. For an early (and brief) argument about affirmative action as reparations, see Feuer 1985.

4. Beyond the Schoolhouse

1. Essays and books on American science policy should be required reading for teacher educators and other university faculty. The short list includes Bush 1945; Steelman 1947. For analysis and commentary, see Atkinson 2015; Blanpied 1998; U.S. Congress, OTA 1991; Feuer 2020a; Sarewitz 1996; and chapter 2 in Feuer 2016. For discussion of alternate views of the meanings of basic and applied science, see Stokes 1997; and Feuer 2014. For reflections on the meanings of "useful" research, see Flexner 2017 (originally published in 1939); and Feuer and Atkinson 2006. It is worth noting that Vannevar Bush made his analysis and recommendations almost a decade before the contemporary classics of

"public goods" theory were developed and published by economists such as Paul Samuelson and Richard Musgrave. See the *Stanford Encyclopedia of Philosophy* for historical review and explication of the core ideas, including reference to education as a classic public good.

2. For discussion of the difference between general and specific skills, the original source is Becker 1964. For analysis through the lens of institutional economics and Oliver Williamson's organizational failures framework, see Feuer, Glick, and Desai 1987.

3. The role of religion in shaping school policy and curricula is beyond the scope of this book, although it pays to keep in mind the religious origins of American education and how its guiding principles were revolutionized during the early nineteenth century. See, for example, Kaestle 1983. Other societies have dealt differently with religion in education. In Israel, for example, for many complex historical and cultural reasons, public education funds flow separately to religious, secular, and Arab schools, which maintain distinctive curricula. The possibility that well-meaning sensitivity to religious and ethnic differences had unintended political and social consequences is worth more focused exploration than possible here.

4. The fact that accountability plays such a dominant role in education politics is further evidence of the links between schooling and democracy. On the role of testing, the historian David Tyack (1974) emphasized the initiation of uniform written examinations during the common-school reform era. For a somewhat contrarian view, see Katz 1968. The evolution of test-based accountability is complex and ongoing. As I suggested in an earlier paper, if political economy is largely about the measurement of externalities, test-based accountability necessitates attention to the externalities of measurement; see Feuer 2010. For a recent compilation of research on methods and meanings of

assessment, see Berman, Feuer, and Pellegrino 2019. An aging but still useful reference is Feuer et al. 1992. On the changing federal role in American education, see Jennings 2015. And for a delightfully readable introduction to the fundamentals of education in democracy, see Phillips 2016.

5. For discussion of the consensus committee processes of the National Academies, see Feuer and Maranto 2010; and various chapters in Feuer, Berman, and Atkinson 2015. On research-practice partnerships, see Easton and Bates 2021. For review of issues pertaining to the uses of evidence in educational practice, see Gitomer and Crouse 2019; and Shavelson and Towne 2002. Work underway at the University of Pennsylvania's Annenberg Center is relevant and potentially worth emulating: see https://annenberg.org /category/civic-engagement/. For information about the Government-University-Industry Research Roundtable, see https://www.nationalacademies.org/guirr/government -university-industry-research-roundtable. On research-practice partnerships, see Coburn, Penvel, and Farrell 2021.

6. Excellent examples of cross-national collaboration include the work of the Center for Universal Education (Brookings) and the Social Science Research Council. See https://www .brookings.edu/center/center-for-universal-education/and https://www.ssrc.org/.

Postscript

1. See *New York Times*, Editorial Board 2022; Stockman 2022; Nichols 2022; Rubin 2022.

2. In yet another reminder of how new information often shows up late, as I was completing this manuscript, I learned that Garrett Hardin held strongly anti-immigrant views and was accused by some commentators for holding eugenicist beliefs about racial differences. See, e.g., Southern Poverty Law Center (n.d.). As disturbed as I am to have been alerted to

these allegations, I nonetheless continue to believe that the "commons" logic has significant value if it is interpreted and used appropriately. I trust readers will understand my misgivings about citing scientists or artists or business leaders who have sullied their reputations with abhorrent politics or behavior. In any case, I am grateful to Forrest Maltzman for bringing the Hardin matter to my attention.

3. The argument has echoes in Hirschman's "possibilism." See Ferraton and Frobert 2017. For an enlightened analysis of the dangers of overreacting to short-term economic trends, see Baumol, Blackman, and Wolff 1989.

REFERENCES

★ ★ ★

Adelman, Jeremy. 2013. *Worldly Philosopher*. Princeton, NJ: Princeton University Press.

Adler, Susan A. 2010. *National Curriculum Standards for Social Studies: A Framework for Teaching, Learning and Assessment*. Brentwood, MD: NCSS Publications.

Alexander, Hanan. 2015. *Reimagining Liberal Education: Affiliation and Inquiry in Democratic Schooling*. New York: Bloomsbury Academic.

Applebaum, Anne. 2020. *Twilight of Democracy: The Seductive Lure of Authoritarianism*. New York: Doubleday.

Arrow, Kenneth. 1963. *Social Choice and Individual Values*. New York: Wiley.

Atkinson, Richard C. 2015. "Vannevar Sets the Stage." In *Past as Prologue: The National Academy of Education at 50*, edited by Michael J. Feuer, Amy I. Berman, and Richard C. Atkinson. Washington, DC: National Academy of Education.

Augier, Mie, and James G. March, eds. 2004. *Models of a Man: Essays in Memory of Herbert A. Simon*. Cambridge, MA: MIT Press.

Barr, R. D., J. Barth, and S. Shermis, 1977. "The Nature and Goals of Social Studies." Arlington, VA: National Council for the Social Studies.

Baum, Sandy, and Michael McPherson. 2022. *Can College Level the Playing Field? Higher Education in an Unequal Society*. Princeton, NJ: Princeton University Press.

Baumol, William J. 2002. *The Free Market Innovation Machine.* Princeton, NJ: Princeton University Press.

Baumol, William J., Sue Anne Batey Blackman, and Edward N. Wolff. 1989. *Productivity and American Leadership: The Long View.* Cambridge, MA: MIT Press.

Becker, Gary. 1964. *Human Capital: A Theoretical and Empirical Analysis, with Special Reference to Education.* New York: Columbia University Press.

Berlin, Isaiah. 1997. *The Proper Study of Mankind: An Anthology of Essays.* London: Chatto and Windus.

Berman, Amy I., Michael J. Feuer, and James W. Pellegrino. 2019. "What Use Is Educational Assessment?" *Annals of the American Academy of Political and Social Science,* May 2019.

Berman, Paul, Martin Peretz, Michael Walzer, and Leon Wieseltier. 2023. "We Are Liberal American Zionists. We stand with Israel's protesters." *Washington Post,* February 2. https://www .washingtonpost.com/opinions/2023/02/02/wieseltier-peretz -berman-walzer-israel-netanyahu/.

Blanpied, William. 1998. "Inventing US Science Policy." *Physics Today* 51, no. 2.

Boorstin, Daniel. 1973. *The Americans, Vol. 3: The Democratic Experience.* New York: Random House.

Bowen, William G., and Derek Bok. 2000. *The Shape of the River: Long-Term Consequences of Considering Race in College and University Admissions.* Princeton, NJ: Princeton University Press.

Braun, Henry, and Judith D. Singer. 2018. "Testing International Assessments: Rankings Get Headlines, but Often Mislead" *Science* 360, no. 6384.

Brest, Paul, and Hal Harvey 2018. *Money Well Spent: A Strategic Plan for Smart Philanthropy.* Stanford, CA: Stanford University Press.

Buchanan, Larry, Quoctrung Bui, and Jugal Patel. 2020. "Black Lives Matter May Be the Largest Movement in U.S. History." *New York Times,* July 3, 2020.

Bush, Vannevar. 1945. *Science, the Endless Frontier: A Report to the President. United States.* Washington, DC: U.S. Government Printing Office.

Carrasco, Maria. 2022. "N.H. Gov. Vetoes Bill Requiring Students to Pass Civics Test." *Inside Higher Education,* February 28, 2022.

Cartwright, Nancy. 2011. "A Philosopher's View of the Long Road from RCTs to Effectiveness." *Lancet* 377, no. 9775.

Carugati, Federica, and Margaret Levi. 2021. *A Moral Political Economy.* Cambridge: Cambridge University Press.

Civics Report Card: Trends in Achievement from 1976 to 1988 at Ages 13 and 17. Achievement in 1988 at Grades 4, 8 and 12; 1990 ASI 4898-29; NAEP Rpt. 19-C-01. 1990.

Claridge, Tristan. 2004. "Social Capital and National Resource Management: An Important Role for Social Capital?" Unpublished thesis, University of Queensland, Brisbane, Australia. https://www.socialcapitalresearch.com/literature/definition/.

Coase, Ronald H. 2013. "The Problem of Social Cost." *Journal of Law and Economics* 56, no. 4.

Coburn, Cynthia, William Penuel, and Caitlin C. Farrell. 2021. "Fostering Educational Improvement with Research-Practice Partnerships." *Kappan* 102, no. 7.

Cochran, Kathryn F. 1997. *Pedagogical Content Knowledge: Teachers' Integration of Subject Matter, Pedagogy, Students, and Learning Environments.* https://narst.org/research-matters/pedagogical-content-knowledge.

Cremin, Lawrence A. 1990. *Popular Education and Its Discontents.* New York: Harper & Row.

Crimmins, Eileen M., Samuel H. Preston, and Barney Cohen, eds. 2011. *Explaining Divergent Levels of Longevity in High-Income Countries.* Washington, DC: National Academies Press.

Crittenden, Jack, and Peter Levine. 2018. "Civic Education" in *The Stanford Encyclopedia of Philosophy,* Fall 2018.

Daniels, Ronald J., with Grant Shreve and Phillip Spector. 2021. *What Universities Owe Democracy.* Baltimore: Johns Hopkins University Press.

Dictionnaire philosophique. 1920. Paris: Ernest Flammarion.

Diliberti, Kay, Ashley Woo, and Julia Kaufman. 2023. "The Missing Infrastructure for Elementary (K–5) Social Studies Instruction." RAND. https://www.rand.org/pubs/research_reports/RRA134 -17.html?utm_source=AdaptiveMailer&utm_medium=email&utm _campaign=7014N000002GAc6QAG&utm_term=00v4N00000k TQLKQA4&org=1674&lvl=100&ite=273466&lea=1828668&ctr =0&par=1&trk=a0w4N000009fC0vQAE.

Dionne, E. J., Jr. 2021. "In the Capitol Nightmare, Democracy Prevailed." *Washington Post*, January 11, 2021.

Du Bois, W. E. B. 1903. "The Talented Tenth." In *The Negro Problem: A Series of Articles by Representative American Negroes of Today.* New York: James Pott.

Dworkin, Ronald. 1998. "Affirming Affirmative Action." *New York Review of Books*, October 22, 1998.

Eastern Michigan University. 2006. "Methods for Teaching Secondary Earth Science, Course Syllabus—Fall 06." https://d32ogoq mya1dw8.cloudfront.net/files/teacherprep/courses/essc-347 -syllabus-fall06.pdf.

Easton, John, and Meg Bates. 2021. "Partnerships in Action: A New RPP Highlights the Field's Evolution." https://wtgrantfoundation .org/partnerships-in-action-a-new-rpp-highlights-the-fields -evolution.

Elliott, Stuart, and Michael Hout, eds. 2011. *Incentives and Test-Based Accountability in Education.* Washington, DC: National Academies Press.

Encyclopedia Britannica. 2023. "Herbert A. Simon." Last updated February 5, 2023. https://www.britannica.com/biography/Herbert -A-Simon.

Fallows, James, and Deborah Fallows. 2018. *Our Towns: A 100,000- Mile Journey into the Heart of America.* New York: Pantheon Books.

Ferraton, Cyrille, and Ludovic Frobert. 2017. "Possibilism in Albert O. Hirschman" *Review of Economic Philosophy* 18, no. 2.

Feuer, Michael J. 1984. Review of *Dismantling America*, by Susan J. Tolchin and Martin Tolchin, and *Rebuilding America*, by Frederick Thayer. *Philadelphia Inquirer*, March 25, 1984.

Feuer, Michael J. 1985. "Zionism as Affirmative Action." *Jewish Frontier*, June/July 1985.

Feuer, Michael J. 2006. *Moderating the Debate*. Cambridge, MA: Harvard Education Press.

Feuer, Michael J. 2010. "Externalities of Testing: Lessons from the Blizzard of 2010." *Measurement: Interdisciplinary Research and Perspectives* 8, no. 2.

Feuer, Michael J. 2012. "No Country Left Behind: Rhetoric and Reality of International Large-Scale Assessment." William H. Angoff Memorial Lecture Series. Princeton, NJ: ETS.

Feuer, Michael J. 2013. "STEM Education: Progress and Prospects." *The Bridge* 43, no. 1 (Spring).

Feuer, Michael J. 2014. "Pure and Applied Science and Pasteur's Quadrant." In *Encyclopedia of Educational Theory and Philosophy*, edited by D. C. Phillips. Thousand Oaks, CA: SAGE Reference.

Feuer, Michael J. 2016. *The Rising Price of Objectivity: Philanthropy, Government, and the Future of Education Research*. Cambridge, MA: Harvard Education Press.

Feuer, Michael J. 2018. "Evidence for Opportunity." *Science* 360, no. 6387.

Feuer, Michael J. 2020a. "The Autonomy and Integrity of Science." *Issues in Science and Technology* 36, no. 4 (Summer).

Feuer, Michael J. 2020b. "In Defense of Economists." *Foreign Affairs* 99, no. 4 (July/August).

Feuer, Michael J. 2020c. "Policy Models in Behavioral and Social Sciences." *ITEMS*, Social Science Research Council. https://items.ssrc.org/covid-19-and-the-social-sciences/policy-models-in-pandemic/policy-models-in-behavioral-and-social-sciences/.

Feuer, Michael J. 2021a. Review of *The American Jewish Philanthropic Complex*, by Lilah Corwin-Berman. *Jewish Journal*, March 10, 2021.

Feuer, Michael J. 2021b. "Science, Civics, and Democracy." *Science* 371, no. 6528.

Feuer, Michael J. 2021c. "The Johnson and Johnson Vaccine Pause and the Challenge of Risk Assessment." https://www.brookings .edu/blog/fixgov/2021/04/28/the-johnson-and-johnson -vaccine-pause-and-the-challenge-of-risk-assessment/.

Feuer, Michael J. 2022. "What Is the One Thing Students Should Leave College Knowing?" *Moment* (Spring).

Feuer, Michael J., and Richard C. Atkinson. 2006. "Absurd Studies of Science's Puzzles Prove Their Worth." *San Jose Mercury News*, July 23, 2006.

Feuer, Michael J., Amy I. Berman, and Richard C. Atkinson, eds. 2015. *Past as Prologue: The National Academy of Education at 50.* Washington, DC: National Academy of Education.

Feuer, Michael J., Robert E. Floden, Naomi Chudowsky, and Judi Ahn, eds. 2013. *Evaluation of Teacher Preparation Programs: Purposes, Methods, and Policy Options.* Washington, DC: National Academy of Education.

Feuer, Michael J., H. Glick, and A. Desai. 1987. "Is Firm-Sponsored Education Viable?" *Journal of Economic Behavior and Organization* 8, no. 1 (Spring).

Feuer, Michael J., and Christina J. Maranto. 2010. "Science Advice as Procedural Rationality: Reflections on the National Research Council." *Minerva* 48, no. 3.

Feuer, Michael, Lisa Towne, Adam Burns, and Manuel Rubio. 1997. "School Choice and the Diversity of Schools: Micromotives and Macroeffects." *Georgetown Public Policy Review* 2, no. 2 (Spring).

Fitzgerald, Julie L., and Marley W. Watkins. 2006. "Parents' Rights in Special Education: The Readability of Procedural Safeguards." *Exceptional Children* 72, no. 4.

Flexner, Abraham. 2017. *The Usefulness of Useless Knowledge.* Princeton, NJ: Princeton University Press.

Friedman, Milton. 1966. "The Methodology of Positive Economics." In *Essays in Positive Economics*. Chicago: University of Chicago Press.

Friedman, Milton, and Rose D. Friedman. 1980. *Free to Choose*. New York: Harcourt Brace Jovanovich.

Gamoran, Adam, Hannah K. Miller, Jeremy E. Fiel, and Jessa Lewis Valentine. 2021. "Social Capital and Student Achievement: An Intervention-Based Test of Theory." *Sociology of Education* 94, no. 4.

Gitomer, Drew, and Kevin Crouse. 2019. "Studying the Use of Research Evidence: A Review of Methods." William T. Grant Foundation.

Glanz, James, and Campbell Robertson. 2020. "Lockdown Delays Cost at Least 36,000 Lives, Data Show." *New York Times*, May 20, 2020.

Goldberg, Michelle. 2020. "Opinion—Four Wasted Years Thinking about Donald Trump." *New York Times*, October 29, 2020.

Goldin, Claudia Dale, and Lawrence F. Katz. 2008. *The Race between Education and Technology*. Cambridge, MA: Harvard University Press.

Graham, David. 2023. "Mexicans Turn Out in Droves to Protest Electoral Overhaul, See Democracy at Risk." https://www.msn.com/en-us/news/world/mexicans-turn-out-in-droves-to-protest-electoral-overhaul-see-democracy-at-risk/ar-AA17YjOK.

Greeley, Andrew M., and Michael Hout. 2006. *The Truth about Conservative Christians*. Chicago: University of Chicago Press.

Greenberg, David. 2022. "The War on Objectivity in American Journalism." *Liberties* 2, no. 3 (Spring).

Gudmundsdottir, Sigrun, and Lee Shulman. 1987. "Pedagogical Content Knowledge in Social Studies." *Scandinavian Journal of Educational Research* 31, no. 2.

Hamilton, Laura S., and Ace Parsi. 2022. "Monitoring Civic Learning Opportunities and Outcomes: Lessons from a Symposium

Sponsored by ETS and Educating for American Democracy."
ETS Research Notes. Princeton, NJ: ETS.

Harari, Yuval. 2023. "They've Forgotten What It Means to Be Jewish." *Times of Israel*. March 6. https://blogs.timesofisrael.com/theyve-forgotten-what-it-means-to-be-jewish/.

Hardin, Garrett. 1968. "The Tragedy of the Commons." *Science* 162, no. 3859.

Hauser, Robert M. 2020. "What Is the Matter with America's Schools?" *Proceedings of the American Philosophical Society*, March 1, 2020.

Hayek, Friedrich A. von. 1969. *Road to Serfdom*. Chicago: University of Chicago Press.

Henderson, James, and Richard E. Quandt. 1958. *Microeconomic Theory*. New York: McGraw-Hill.

Hess, Diana E., and Paula McAvoy. 2014. *The Political Classroom*. New York: Routledge.

Hirschman, Albert O. 1970. *Exit, Voice, and Loyalty: Responses to Decline in Firms, Organizations, and States*. Cambridge, MA: Harvard University Press.

Hirschman, Albert O. 1991. *The Rhetoric of Reaction: Perversity, Futility, Jeopardy*. Cambridge, MA: Harvard University Press.

Hirschman, Albert O. 1992. *Rival Views of Market Society and Other Recent Essays*. Cambridge, MA: Harvard University Press.

Hochschild, Jennifer L., and Nathan B. Scovronick. 2003. *The American Dream and the Public Schools*. Oxford: Oxford University Press.

House, James S. 2015. *Beyond Obamacare: Life, Death, and Social Policy*. New York: Russell Sage Foundation.

Jarrell, Randall. 1958. "The Taste of the Age." *Saturday Evening Post*, July 26, 1958.

Jennings, Jack. 2015. *Presidents, Congress, and the Public Schools: The Politics of Education Reform*. Cambridge, MA: Harvard Education Press.

Jones, Lyle, and Ingram Olkin, eds. 2004. *The Nation's Report Card: Evolution and Perspectives*. Bloomington, IN: Phi Delta Kappa Education Foundation.

Kaestle, Carl F. 1983. *Pillars of the Republic*. New York: Hill & Wang.

Kaestle, Carl F. 2000. "Toward a Political Economy of Citizenship: Historical Perspectives on the Purposes of Common Schools." In *Rediscovering the Democratic Purposes of Education*, edited by Lorraine M. McDonnell, P. Michael Timpane, and Roger Benjamin. Lawrence: University Press of Kansas.

Kahlenberg, Richard D. 2007. *Tough Liberal: Albert Shanker and the Battles over Schools, Unions, Race, and Democracy*. New York: Columbia University Press.

Kamarck, Elaine. 2021. "Did Trump Damage American Democracy?" *FixGov* (blog) July 9, 2021. Washington, DC: Brookings Institution. https://search.proquest.com/docview/2550051200.

Katz, Michael B. 1968. *The Irony of Early School Reform*. Cambridge, MA: Harvard University Press.

King, Martin Luther, III. 2021. "Mobilize Everyday People to Fight Republican Attacks on Voting, Just Like in 1965: MLK III." *USA Today*, August 6, 2021.

Kitcher, Philip. 2022. "Education and the Economic Menace." *Liberties* 2, no. 2 (Winter).

Klein, Joel I., Condoleezza Rice, and Julia Levy. 2012. *U.S. Education Reform and National Security*. Council on Foreign Relations.

Kramer, Margaret. 2019. "A Timeline of Key Supreme Court Cases on Affirmative Action." *New York Times*, March 30, 2019.

Krugman, Paul R., and Robin Wells. 2015. *Macroeconomics*. New York: Worth.

Lagemann, Ellen Condliffe. 1989. *The Politics of Knowledge: The Carnegie Corporation, Philanthropy, and Public Policy*. Middletown, CT: Wesleyan University Press.

Landwehr, Claudia, and Armin Schäfer. 2020. "Populist, Technocratic, and Authoritarian Responses to Covid-19." Social Science Research Council, *Items*, July 23, 2020.

Lapin, Andrew. 2021. "Radioactive: The Father Coughlin Story." *Tablet* (podcast), October 5, 2021. https://www.tabletmag.com/podcasts/radioactive.

Lemann, Nicholas. 1996. "Kicking in Groups." *Atlantic*, April 1996.

Lepore, Jill. 2022. "Why the School Wars Still Rage." *New Yorker*, March 14, 2022.

Lesh, Bruce A. 2011. *"Why Won't You Just Tell Us the Answer?" Teaching Historical Thinking in Grades 7–12*. Portland, ME: Stenhouse.

Lewis, Jack. 1985. "The Birth of EPA." *EPA Journal* (November).

Lewis, Michael. 2017. *The Undoing Project*. New York: Norton.

Lilla, Mark, Ronald Dworkin, and Robert Silvers, eds. 2001. *The Legacy of Isaiah Berlin*. New York: New York Review of Books, 2001.

Lindbeck, Assar. 1992. *Nobel Lectures in Economic Sciences*. River Edge, NJ: World Scientific.

Lindblom, Charles Edward. 1980. *Politics and Markets*. New York: Basic Books.

Lipsey, Richard George. 1971. *An Introduction to Positive Economics*. London: Weidenfeld and Nicolson.

Liptak, Adam, and Anemona Hartocollis. 2022. "Supreme Court Will Hear Challenge to Affirmative Action at Harvard and U.N.C." *New York Times*, January 24, 2022.

List, John A. 2022. *The Voltage Effect: How to Make Good Ideas Great and Great Ideas Scale*. New York: Currency.

Lopez, G. 2023. "The End of Affirmative Action." *New York Times*, June 30, 2023.

Lozada, Carlos. 2020. *What Were We Thinking: A Brief Intellectual History of the Trump Era*. New York: Simon & Schuster.

Lozada, Carlos. 2022. "How to Strangle Democracy While Pretending to Engage in It." *New York Times*, October 20, 2022.

Maddow, Rachel. 2022. *Rachel Maddow Presents: Ultra* (podcast). MSNBC.

McDonnell, Lorraine, 2000. "Defining Democratic Purposes." In *Rediscovering the Democratic Purposes of Education*. Lawrence: University Press of Kansas.

McDonnell, Lorraine, P. Michael Timpane, and Roger Benjamin, eds. 2000. *Rediscovering the Democratic Purposes of Education*. Lawrence: University Press of Kansas.

Mendes-Flohr, Paul. 2022. "Why Is America Different? The Price and Promise of Jewish Emancipation." *Sources* 2, no. 1 (Spring).

Milbank, Dana. 2022. *The Destructionists: The Twenty-Five-Year Crack-Up of the Republican Party*, New York: Doubleday.

Mirel, Jeffrey. 2010. *Patriotic Pluralism*. Cambridge, MA: Harvard University Press.

Moffatt, Mike. 2019. "Breakdown of Positive and Negative Externalities in a Market." ThoughtCo., April 20, 2019. https://www.thoughtco.com/definition-of-externality-1146092.

Mufson, Steven. 2021. "Nobel Winner's Evolution from 'Dark Realist' to Just Plain Realist on Climate Change." *Washington Post*, June 14, 2021.

Mullis, I. 2019. "White Paper on 50 Years of NAEP Use: Where NAEP Has Been and Where It Should Go Next." Boston: Boston College.

Murnane, Richard, and Sean F. Reardon. 2018. "Long-Term Trends in Private School Enrollment by Family Income." *AERA Open* 4, no. 1.

Murray, Charles, and Christopher Jencks. 1985. "'Losing Ground': An Exchange." *New York Review of Books*, October 24, 1985.

"NAEP Report Card: Civics." 2023. https://www.nationsreportcard.gov/civics/results/achievement/.

National Academy of Education. 2022. *Brief of the National Academy of Education as Amicus Curiae in Support of Respondents*, 2022 (accessible at https://naeducation.wpenginepowered.com/wp-content/uploads/2022/08/NAEd-Supreme-Court-brief-race-conscious-admissions-policies.pdf).

Nelson, Murray, ed. 1994. *The Social Studies in Secondary Education [Microform]: A Reprint of the Seminal 1916 Report, with Annotations and Commentaries*. Bloomington, IN: ERIC Clearinghouse for Social Studies/Social Science Education.

New York Times. 2022. "Interview: Why the Nobel-Winning Economist Amartya Sen Recommends 'King Lear.'" January 6, 2022.

New York Times, Editorial Board. 2022. "Political Violence Is Threatening Our Democracy," November 6, 2022.

Next Generation Science Standards. n.d. Accessed February 23, 2023. https://www.nextgenscience.org/developing-standards/developing-standards.

Nichols, Tom. 2022. "Deniers Denied." *Atlantic*, November 9, 2022.

Niemi, Richard G., and Jane Junn. 1998. *Civic Education*. New Haven, CT: Yale University Press.

Nordhaus, William. 2021. *The Spirit of Green: The Economics of Collisions and Contagions in a Crowded World*. Princeton, NJ: Princeton University Press.

Olson, Mancur. 1965 and 1971. *The Logic of Collective Action*. Cambridge, MA: Harvard University Press.

Oren, Michael. 2023. "Judicial Reform: Right Problem, Wrong Solution." *The Times of Israel*, February 12. https://blogs.timesofisrael.com/the-proposed-judicial-reform-addresses-the-right-issue-in-the-wrong-way/.

Packer, George. 2021. *Last Best Hope: America in Crisis and Renewal*. New York: Farrar, Straus and Giroux.

Packer, George. 2022. "Review—A New Book Imagines a Looming Civil War over the Very Meaning of America." *Washington Post*, March 27, 2022.

Parker, Walter, ed. 1996. *Educating the Democratic Mind*. Albany: State University of New York Press.

Pew Research Center. 2014. "Religious Landscapes Study." https://www.pewresearch.org/religion/religious-landscape-study/#religions.

Pew Research Center. 2022. "45% of Americans Say U.S. Should Be a 'Christian Nation.'" https://www.pewresearch.org/religion/2022/10/27/45-of-americans-say-u-s-should-be-a-christian-nation/.

Phillips, D. C. 2016. *A Companion to John Dewey's Democracy and Education*. Chicago: University of Chicago Press.

Phillips, David, and Kimberly Ochs. 2003. "Processes of Policy Borrowing in Education: Some Explanatory and Analytical Devices." *Comparative Education* 39, no. 4.

Public Policy Polling. 2016. National Survey Results. https://www.socialsecurityworks.org/wp-content/uploads/2016/10/National Results.pdf.

Public Religion Research Institute. 2023. "A Christian Nation? Understanding the Threat of Christian Nationalism to American Democracy and Culture." https://www.prri.org/research/a-christian -nation-understanding-the-threat-of-christian-nationalism-to -american-democracy-and-culture/.

Putnam, Robert D. 1995. "Bowling Alone: America's Declining Social Capital." *Journal of Democracy* 6, no. 1.

Putnam, Robert D. 2000. *Bowling Alone: The Collapse and Revival of American Community*. New York: Simon & Schuster.

Putnam, Robert D. 2020. *The Upswing: How America Came Together a Century Ago and How We Can Do It Again*. New York: Simon & Schuster.

Rai, Tage, and Brad Wible. 2020. "In Flux and Under Threat." *Science* 369, no. 6508.

Ravitch, Diane. 1974 *The Great School Wars: New York City, 1805–1973*. New York: Basic Books.

Raymond, Macke, et al. https://credo.stanford.edu/report-finder /charter-study/.

Redman, Eric. 2000. *The Dance of Legislation: An Insider's Account of the Workings of the United States Senate*. Seattle: University of Washington Press.

Remnick, David. 2020. "The Coronavirus and the Threat within the White House." *New Yorker*, October 12.

Reich, Rob. 2013. "What Are Foundations For?" *Boston Review* 38, no. 2.

Reuben, Julie A. 1997. "Beyond Politics: Community Civics and the Redefinition of Citizenship in the Progressive Era." *History of Education Quarterly* 37, no. 4.

Roberts, Siobhan. 2020. "'The Pandemic Is a Prisoner's Dilemma Game.'" *New York Times*, December 23, 2020.

Robert Wood Johnson Foundation. 2014. "Going Beyond Clinical Walls: Solving Complex Problems," report of the Institute for Clinical Systems Improvement. https://www.icsi.org/wp-content/uploads/2019/08/1.SolvingComplexProblems_BeyondClinicalWalls.pdf.

Romer, Paul. 2020. "The Dismal Kingdom: Do Economists Have Too Much Power?" *Foreign Affairs* 99, no. 2.

Romney, Mitt. 2022. "The Democrats Have Ventured Deep into Hyperbole and Hysteria." https://www.romney.senate.gov/romney-democrats-have-ventured-deep-hyperbole-and-hysteria/.

Rotberg, Iris C., and Joshua L. Glazer, eds. 2018. *Choosing Charters*. New York: Teachers College Press.

Rubin, Beth C. 2011. *Making Citizens: Transforming Civic Learning for Diverse Social Studies Classrooms*. New York: Routledge.

Rubin, Jennifer. 2022. "7 Reasons to Be Optimistic about the Future of Democracy." *Washington Post*, November 13, 2022.

Rucker, Philip, Ashley Parker, Josh Dawsey, and Amy Gardner. 2020. "20 Days of Fantasy and Failure: Inside Trump's Quest to Overturn the Election." *Washington Post*, November 28, 2020.

Ryan, Katherine, and Lorrie Shepard. 2008. *The Future of Test-Based Educational Accountability*. New York: Routledge.

Sacks, Rabbi Jonathan. 2004. *A Letter in the Scroll*. New York: Free Press.

Samuelson, Paul A. 1955. *Foundations of Economic Analysis*. Cambridge, MA: Harvard University Press.

Sarewitz, Daniel. 1996. *Frontiers of Illusion: Science, Technology, and the Politics of Progress*. Philadelphia, PA: Temple University Press.

Scheffler, Israel. 2003. "The Concept of the Educated Person, with some Applications to Jewish Education." In *Visions of Jewish Education*, edited by Seymour Fox, Israel Scheffler, and Daniel Marom. Cambridge: Cambridge University Press.

Schelling, Thomas C. 1978. *Micromotives and Macrobehavior*. New York: Norton.

Schneider, Donald O. 1994. *Expectations of Excellence: Curriculum Standards for Social Studies*. Washington, DC: National Council for the Social Studies.

Schuman, Michael. 2022. "Behold, Emperor Xi." *Atlantic*, October 13, 2022.

Shavelson, Richard, and Lisa Towne, eds. 2002. *Scientific Research in Education*. Washington, DC: National Academies Press.

Shulman, Lee S. 1986. "Those Who Understand: Knowledge Growth in Teaching." *Educational Researcher* 15, no. 2.

Simon, Herbert. 1976. "From Substantive to Procedural Rationality." In *Method and Appraisal in Economics*, edited by Spiro Latsis. Cambridge: Cambridge University Press.

Simon, Herbert. 1978. "Rationality as Process and as Product of Thought." *American Economic Review* 68, no. 2.

Smith, Adam. 1971 (1759). *The Theory of Moral Sentiments*. New York: Garland Pub.

Smith, Adam. 2003 (1776). *The Wealth of Nations*. New York: Bantam Classic.

Socken, Paul. 2022. "And the Winner of the Nobel Prize is . . . Jewish!" *Jewish Journal*, April 29, 2022.

Southern Poverty Law Center. n.d. "Garrett Hardin." Accessed February 24, 2023. https://www.splcenter.org/fighting-hate/extremist-files/individual/garrett-hardin.

Snyder, Timothy. 2017. *On Tyranny: Twenty Lessons from the Twentieth Century*. New York: Tim Duggan Books.

Steelman, John Roy. 1980 (1947). *Science and Public Policy*. New York: Arno.

Stiglitz, Joseph E. 1997. *Principles of Microeconomics*. 2nd ed. New York: Norton.

Stockman, Farah. 2022. "This Group Has $100 Million and a Big Goal: To Fix America." *New York Times*, November 6, 2022.

Stokes, Donald E. 1997. *Pasteur's Quadrant*. Washington, DC: Brookings Institution Press.

Stout, Cathryn, and Thomas Wilburn. 2022. "CRT Map: Efforts to restrict teaching racism and bias have multiplied across the U.S." https://www.chalkbeat.org/22525983/map-critical-race-theory-legislation-teaching-racism

Swan, Kathy, John Lee, and S. G. Grant, 2018. *Inquiry Design Model: Building Inquiries in Social Studies*. Silver Spring, MD: National Council for the Social Studies.

Thaler, Richard H., and Cass R. Sunstein. 2009. *Nudge*. New York: Penguin Books.

Thorp, Holden. 2023a. "The College Board Can't Be Trusted." https://www.science.org/doi/10.1126/science.adi4588.

Thorp, Holden. 2023b. "Words Yes, Actions Unlikely." https://www.science.org/doi/10.1126/science.adh4603.

Thunberg, Greta. 2019. "The Disarming Case to Act Right Now on Climate Change." https://www.ted.com/talks/greta_thunberg_the_disarming_case_to_act_right_now_on_climate_change.

Tierney, John. 2009. "Debating the Longevity Gap." *New York Times*, September 23, 2009.

Torney-Purta, Judith, Rainier Lehmann, Hans Oswald, and Wolfram Schulz. 2001. *Citizenship and Education in Twenty-Eight Countries*. Amsterdam: IEA, International Association for the Evaluation of Educational Achievement.

Tyack, David B. 1974. *The One Best System*. Cambridge, MA: Harvard University Press.

Tyack, David, and Larry Cuban. 1995. *Tinkering Toward Utopia: A Century of Public School Reform*. Cambridge, MA: Harvard University Press.

Tyler, Ralph. 2011. "From *The NAEP Primer*: A Technical History of NAEP." https://nces.ed.gov/nationsreportcard/about/newnaephistory.aspx.

U.S. Congress, Office of Technology Assessment. 1991. *Federally Funded Research: Decisions for a Decade*, OTA-SET-490. Washington, DC: U.S. Government Printing Office.

U.S. Congress, Office of Technology Assessment. 1992. *Testing in American Schools: Asking the Right Questions*, OTA-SET-519. Washington, DC: U.S. Government Printing Office.

Wagner, J., Anderson, N., Wang, A., Berman, M., and Vazquez, M. 2023. "Supreme Court Ruling Restricts Affirmative Action in College Admissions." *Washington Post*. June 29. https://www.washingtonpost.com/education/2023/06/29/supreme-court-student-loan-forgiveness-affirmative-action/.

Walzer, Michael. 2004. "What Does It Mean to Be an American?" *Social Research* 71, no. 3 (Fall).

Williams, James H., and Laura C. Engel. 2013. "Testing to Rank, Testing to Learn, Testing to Improve: An Introduction and Overview." *Research in Comparative and International Education* 8, no. 3.

Williamson, Oliver E. 1975. *Markets and Hierarchies: Analysis and Antitrust Implications. A Study in the Economics of Internal Organization.* New York: Free Press.

Willick, Jason. 2023. "How Israel's Culture War Turns America's Upside-Down." *Washington Post*. March 5. https://www.washingtonpost.com/opinions/2023/03/05/israel-supreme-court-protests-religion/.

World Population Review. 2023. "Standard of Living by Country | Quality of Life by Country." https://worldpopulationreview.com/country-rankings/standard-of-living-by-country.

INDEX

★ ★ ★

taxes, 26, 31, 119, 133–34
teacher education: on civics education, 18–20, 22–23, 77–78, 93–94, 98–108, 136–41, 151–52; collaborative and interdisciplinary approach to, 19–20, 22–24, 136–46, 152; on collective action, 136, 138–39; on data science education, 106–8; formal and experiential instruction in, 100; partnerships beyond academia for, 19–20, 23–24, 141–46; on STEM education, 22, 102–8, 137, 139–41, 142; syllabi for, 22, 99–103, 107–8, 138–41
think tanks, 23, 30, 36, 147, 151
totalitarianism, 15, 58. *See also* authoritarianism; autocracy
tragedy of the commons, 15, 21, 51–52, 53, 55–60, 115, 149

transaction costs, 32, 39, 121
Trump administration, 2, 5–6, 41, 45, 85
Tyack, David, 91

unintended consequences, 53–54
university-based civic education, 17–20, 22–24, 136–46, 151–52. *See also* teacher education
University of North Carolina, 125
Usdan, Mike, 18n

Voltaire, 38
voting, 28, 53, 150. *See also* elections

Walzer, Michael, 66
Whitehead, Alfred North, 51
Williamson, Oliver, 56, 57n